THE PHANTOM OF THE GREAT HOUSE

By

R OSELLE T HOMPSON

EAGLE PUBLICATIONS

Published by Eagle Publications
P O Box 73374, London W3 3FZ, England.
A Paperback Original

First published in the United Kingdom in 2021

Text copyright © 2021 Roselle Thompson

The right of Roselle Thompson to be identified as the Author of this work has been asserted by her.

ISBN 978-1-8381068-4-3

A CIP catalogue record for this book is available from the British Library
All Rights Reserved
This book is sold subject to the condition that it shall not, by way of trade or otherwise, be lent, hired out or otherwise circulated in any form of binding or cover other than that in which it is published. No part of this publication may be reproduced, stored in a retrieval system, or transmitted in any form or by any means (electronic, mechanical, photocopying, recording or otherwise) without the prior written permission of Eagle Publications.

All paper used by Eagle Publications is SFI (Sustainable Forestry Initiative) and PEFC (Programme for the Endorsement of Forest Certification Schemes) Certified.
This is a work of fiction. Names, characters, incidents and dialogues are products of the author's imagination or are used fictitiously. Any resemblance to actual people, living or dead, events or locales is entirely coincidental.

Printed in the United Kingdom and United States by
Lightning Source for Eagle Publishers

www.eaglepublications.org.uk

CONTENTS

Introduction	ii – xli
Notes to the Introduction	xlii - xlv
Characters	
ACT 1 SCENE 1: Long Time We Doh Fete Like This!	1
ACT 1 SCENE 2: A Fortune From Far Away	8
ACT 1 SCENE 3: The Phantom Is Stirring	12
ACT 2 SCENE 1: Chasing The Phantom	16
ACT 2 SCENE 2: Young, With Guts Like Cobo	19
ACT 2 SCENE 3: The Phantom Rides Again!	23
ACT 2 SCENE 4: What You Head Lead You To Do, You Backside Go Pay For It	28
ACT 2 SCENE 5: Papa Mwen, Ca C'est Comess Oui!	31
ACT 3 SCENE 1: Obeah Wedding Bells Don't Chime	45
ACT 3 SCENE 2: Let Sleeping Dogs Lie	50
ACT 3 SCENE 3: Fattening Frog For Snake	53
ACT 3 SCENE 4: The Mad Woman In The Attic	56
ACT 4 SCENE 1: Meeting The Past In The Present	64
ACT 4 SCENE 2: Laugh And Cry Does Live In The Same House	73
ACT 4 SCENE 3: Doh Count Egg In Fowl Bottom	76
ACT 5 SCENE 1: Moon Run Faas Till Day Ketch 'Im	81
ACT 5 SCENE 2: Hang Yu Basket Whe You Can Reach It	83
ACT 5 SCENE 3: When Coco Ripe It Mus' Bus'!	86
GLOSSARY	**95**

INTRODUCTION

The *Phantom of the Great House* play is a Caribbean story, based on a *Great House* on Carriere Estate, St. Andrews Parish, in the island of Grenada. Being part of the lore or orally expressed artform of the folks, makes it a Grenadian folktale. The *Great House* story encapsulates the main narrative of this Play, and forms the [1]*mise-en-abîme,* which presents subtexts as well as signifiers within the text, that mirror each other on different levels. In other words, with this literary technique, the tale presents the historic *Great House* as the frame story or main narrative, from which the reader is taken to other related tales within the text, that repeatedly mirror the main theme and are inextricably linked to it. For example, exploring the background to the *Great House*, presents Stella's personal tale, as the main tale, which highlights thematic concerns that open up a window on the following sub-texts:

1. The tale of the *Great House* and its past operation in the island, is **local folk history**. It is fused with the lives and history of the local folks since they were integral to **maintaining a planter-class family of colonials** and their post-colonial activities in the island. Arriving with a colonizer's arrogance, the McDonalds subsequent desire for the affection of the locals, gradually take on the 'self-loathing' of the colonized. This is evident in Mr. McDonald being cuckolded by his wife; stemming from her admiration, sexual attraction, and subsequent illegitimate pregnancy for a native man.

2. The *Great House's* **past presents the history of various waves of colonisation in the island**, embodied in the folks' ways of life. Subsequently, they transmit corresponding folktales, that highlight a history of the island. It indicts subjugation as an inherently imperial ideology, structured by principles of hierarchy. However, folk aesthetics binds

INTRODUCTION   iii

the islanders together as a little community, marred by forced subordination and the effects of colonization.

3. The story presents the role of the **Planter-Class, colonials in the island** and their assets in a post-colonial setting. (Evidenced by the English Planters – the McDonalds, and the Kents before them). This highlights the notion that the comfort and attractiveness of their way of life is inseparable from the violence that their imperial expansion for political and economic imperatives does, to those it seeks to oppress.

4. *Stella's story is a journey of self-discovery*, which interrogates the background and legacy of an heirloom, that has been passed down to her. This story presents a constructive engagement with the problems of race, as well as the diaspora, in a story that goes beyond the dualist thinking of white colonial master versus natives in the Caribbean islands.

5. The *politics of white male hegemony, versus black male powerlessness*. Evidenced by Mr. McDonalds *(Alex to a lesser degree)*, vs. Christopher, Little Chris, the government Minister, and the all-male *Chorus* group. More specifically, the natural-historical classification of Self vs Others, provide a rationale for colonial domination since it ranked the races by a supposed perception of their civilisation.

6. The *synthesis of language and cultural traditions* in the Caribbean island, and its corresponding polylingual environment; input by French, British (*English, Irish, Scottish & Welsh*) colonials, as well as African and indigenous languages, have implications for society in the present.

7. The *influence of colonial spiritual beliefs, (seen in English and French-originated folktales), as well as the strong*

INTRODUCTION

>   *African spiritual input (seen in Mama Lola's obeah practices),* in the island, foreground the basis for "fear;" which can be interpreted on different levels.

8. **Migration to and from the Caribbean** and the *"push"* and *"pull"* factors, that influence the exit of younger generations from the Caribbean to metropolitan cities abroad. Exiting the island becomes an aesthetic mission, while the subject of who has set the standards and judges aesthetic value, is white and European.

9. **Post-colonial insecurities among the older folks,** influenced by a diminishing interest in folklore, by the younger generation, signals a corresponding 'instability' of folk culture. This concern is presented as *a lament* throughout the play, due to the socio-economic and culturally changing landscape. The fact that modernisation and changes in group interactions have impinged on the social participatory role of the ageing in society.

10. The Play also highlights various **functions of the folktale, the role of the storytelling tradition in society,** and **the existence of a Caribbean gothic tradition** within the Caribbean Canon.

The Colonial Background

The background to colonisation in the *Phantom of the Great House*, began with Africans being raided and traded on the African continent, and then shipped via the Transatlantic slave crossing, to work as slaves on plantations in the Caribbean generally, from the 15th to the mid-19th century. (Specifically, in Grenada's case it began in the 17th century). It was a period that eventually resulted in rebellion, emancipation, and post-emancipation periods of trading, that saw the development of a planter-class of rich, sugar barons, still maintaining their assets on the island.

Prior to colonisation, the Tri-island State of Grenada, (*Grenada, Carriacou, and Petite Martinique*), was populated by Caribs and Arawaks; Amerindians from South America, from as early as 3600BC.

INTRODUCTION

These indigenous peoples, having lived on the island for centuries, evolved their own civilisation, until in 1649, when a French expedition from Martinique, founded a permanent settlement in Grenada. The French signed a peace treaty with *Kairouane,* the Carib Chief, but this resulted in conflict between them. However, it is widely known that many of the Caribs and Arawaks throughout the Caribbean region, resisted colonisation; some fought colonisers, others chose to either maim or kill themselves, rather than be caught and forced into slavery; thereby drastically depleting their numbers.

Warfare continued during the 1600's between the French and the Caribs from other neighbouring islands, such as Dominica, St. Vincent and the Grenadines. Having established themselves as controllers of the island, the French named Grenada, *La Grenade* and created plantations for sugar-cane production, using African slaves. However, The British, having assessed their lucrative trade, captured Grenada from the French, during the Seven Years War in 1762. Then via the [2]*Treaty of Paris*, in 1763, Grenada was formally ceded to Britain. It was the British acquisition from France in 1763, that gave Scottish Highlanders the opportunity to really establish a footing in the Caribbean, including Grenada. Hence, use of the family name, McDonalds, in the *Phantom of the Great House* is apt, since it highlights Scottish engagement in a deeply exploitative, slave-based economy, that would lead to an expanded culture of enterprise and prosperity for Scotland. This did two things for the British empire; satisfy Britain's deep concern for the socio-economic and cultural survival of the Highlands from a domestic perspective; whilst encouraging them to engage in imperial pursuits. However, just over a decade later, the French re-captured the island during the American Revolutionary War in 1779.

Such was the fierce pursuit and competition between European countries to conquer other lands, Britain fought the French and regained the island via another treaty; the [3]*Treaty of Versailles* in 1783. Having regained control of Grenada, the British grew the economy by transporting African slaves, and establishing the Slave Trade until 1834. Therefore, the various waves of colonisers to the island, with their own administrators, had mixed with the slave population, thus creating offspring that were known as [4]*Mulattos* (a term used to describe people of mixed black and white ancestry); thus, creating a [5]**Creole** identity, (British and French), in the mixed ancestry of Grenada.

Later in 1834, with the abolition of slavery, a further influx of migrants, Indian indentured labourers, were brought into the island by the British in 1857, with their own varieties of culture and languages. This group was followed by European indentured servants, including French, Spanish, Portuguese, British (e.g., Irish, Scottish, and Welsh), Libyans - all joined Grenada's already mixed cultural environment; hence the resultant fusion of cultures in the island.

The most common groups of enslaved Africans in Grenada were Ghanaian Fante (Akan) people with their population of 19%, constituted the single largest African tribe, followed by Yoruba and Igbos at 34%. Mixed black and European ancestry (Mulatto are 13%) made up 95% of the Grenadian population according to 2012 census, whilst black Grenadians make up 82% of the population, of the Tri-island State.

The Caribbean Storytelling Tradition

Caribbean folktales were orally transmitted beliefs, myths, and tales from one generation to another, originating (though not exclusively) from Africa, told by the slaves who were brought to the region. The folk tales were mainly about beliefs, myths, and practices of African-Caribbean people. This is why some tales have religious figures or supernatural folklore figures, which possess characteristics that are identical to those of African deities. But, this body of African folklore has been synthesised and influenced by English, French and to a lesser degree, Spanish and Dutch colonisers, who brought their own brand of lore into the Caribbean region. These different types of folk lore found expression in the Caribbean, seen as the *new* environment, were later used in situations that warranted use of a tale as a kind of coded message; such as in situations that needed instilling caution, warning,

INTRODUCTION vii

applying cunning, courage or good sense. Subsequently, these tales which were fused with African lore, had a new function and expression in the Caribbean environment. Today, there are vestiges of various colonial inputs, (as seen in the play's linguistic framework), in addition to those that have been brought by Slaves to the region. These have created many types of renewed characters like *Anancy;* the trickster spider; formally an Akan god.

The existence of Caribbean folktales shows how, over the hundreds of years of slavery, these tales have been indelibly etched in the subconscious of the Caribbean people, so that transmitting the stories from one generation to the other, symbolises the transference of a kind of Caribbean cultural heirloom. History has shown that belief in the folk characters cannot be easily forgotten, in the same way that the history of the people cannot be obliterated. It is for these reasons that these stories find expressions within the Caribbean landscape, and evidence a fusion of Africa's deep consciousness within the people's psyche, through their recreated lore. These tales have been kept alive by the older generation; those who have transmitted them to surviving groups of Caribbean people. But with the passage of time, as well as the older generation, many have ceased the practice of the traditional storytelling.

This tradition with which the old folks have grown up, is an age-old traditional experience. These *"crick-crack!"* [6]story-telling sessions are framed as follows: It is a warm, moonlit night in a Caribbean village as crickets and fireflies dance in the tropical air. Under a damsel tree in a neighbour's yard, eager village children gather for a folk event. The nearby trees, casting giant shadows around them, create a mood of togetherness, expectation, and camaraderie. Everyone is seated on the ground, in a semi-circle and a Caribbean folktale, from one of the old folks, is told to the delight and participation of its eager audience.

However, in modern times, the traditional mode of transmission, images of the folks and the physical story-telling sessions, have diminished. This dilemma, has been blamed on succeeding generations of Caribbean youths, both in the region and abroad, who seem to have lost touch with this once vibrant traditional experience. In fact, many Caribbean youths (especially those in the Diaspora), are mostly oblivious of the very existence of the language, lore and stories of the past. As a result of this situation, there is a need to preserve the tales and their essence in Caribbean culture, as well as their meaning in Caribbean people's lives. But times have changed and there is a suggestion, voiced by Anancy in the **Chorus**, (Act 5 Sc 3), that the environment must adapt to the changes, in order for this aspect of the cultural tradition to survive. However, despite adaptation of new methods of transmitting the tales and ensuring their longevity for succeeding generations, in the 21st century, with the use of technology and electronic devices, there is still a sense of erosion of the traditions embodied in storytelling sessions, that makes the *'live'* method of transmission, seem anachronistic in modern times.

    In the **Phantom of the Great House**, (Act 2 Sc5), this concern is articulated by each member of the **Chorus**, *(Anancy, Cricket, Firefly, Frog, and Papa Bois)*. These night-time creatures, symbolically, represent the older generation, or those who have, and continue to participate in this cultural activity. Their first-hand experiences of the transmission of the language and lore of the people, make them credible witnesses and judges of the waning nature of this cultural stabiliser. Their evaluation of the status of the folktales and the peoples' attitudes to them are presented as *a lament*, that seeks to interrogate their dilemma, as a clarion call to revitalise interest in the story-telling tradition. Simultaneously, as a **Chorus**, they also appear to recognise the need to adapt to the changing environment. Given the 'disappearance' of the folks from the traditional story-telling setting, Anancy and Cricket in Act 5 Sc 3, highlight the interest shown in the folktales by academia, may suggest that all is not yet lost. Strategically, the tales' *'permanent'* formats, would enable masses to be acquainted with them, in ways that do not necessarily need a physical gathering of people on a moonlit night, because technology makes it possible for individuals to both *hear* and *see* the tales, in the comfort and privacy of their own spaces, globally.

INTRODUCTION

One element of 'advancement' in the landscape that impacts on storytelling at night, is presented as the pervasive nature of electricity everywhere. In Act 2 Sc 5, Cricket claims, it has robbed them of the storytelling aura. Added to the loss of the story-telling atmosphere, are other characteristics of the old format of transmission, these characteristics were helpful in creating meaning. They took the form of voicing approval, especially from live responses; ensured camaraderie or solidarity, in the live atmosphere among the fellowship of brothers and sisters; generated a heightened sense of significance, expressiveness, and group actions. Therefore, the *group* dynamics are lost through the *solitary* experience of listening to a recorded story. Throughout the play, this sense of loss is demonstrated by the **Chorus**' alternative, isolated, activities; playing dominoes by themselves, having a cook-up or just [7]*liming*; as a push against current 21st century's "indoor generation" ideals.

Evident in Caribbean storytelling are characteristics that highlight a blend of cultural and linguistic influences. These are shown by the inclusion of colour, humour, folk-wisdom, different language registers and thought-processes, which suggest there is still the transmission of caution, verbal defence, and attempts to instil good sense via their didactic aims and objectives. However, it is the African input which has undoubtedly contributed to most of the Caribbean region's folklore, (being the largest racial group in the region). At times these show extensions of supernatural folklore figures, with characteristics that are identical to African deities. For example, *Anansi* or *Anancy*, (often called *Brer Anancy)*, is originally an Akan God who will chastise you in African folk lore but in the Caribbean, he is a cunning spider whose job is to outwit others in order to survive; as a kind of exemplar for slaves against their fearful colonial masters. However, in a post-colonial context, embodied in the concerns articulated by the **Chorus** in this Play, is a lack of understanding by the younger generation, of the past linkages and relevance of the tales to the present. This is echoed in Act 2 Sc 5, when Frog laments, "*...every time I try to tell* *my tadpoles about the old folktales, they laugh at me and say they never hear 'bout any storytellin' by no folks."*

The group's concerns draw attention to the inter-generational strife between the older generation's ways of thinking; whose memory and discourse are still linked to their past. This is squared against a point of divergence among the emerging younger generations, which seem to suggest they are more ready to dismiss the tales as being irrelevant to their current existence. Possible reasons could range from a question of identity, the notion of a sense of place, culture, and its representation, as well as the relevance of these, to their lifestyles. Christopher tells Stella that real life, one of advancement, is best found abroad; specifically for him, it will be achieved by his migration to America, (Act 2 Sc 2).

Ultimately, the story concludes that a denial of the relevance of folk wisdom, has resulted in adverse repercussions for the young, that draw attention to the following: the story's background, the lack of transmitting folk wisdom amongst the young. It challenges them to make the body of orally transmitted texts readily accessible to emerging generations, who are expected to ensure their continuation in the future. However, despite its folkloric function, linguistically and culturally, the tale of the *Great House* is also presented as a gothic one since it embodies the characteristic features of Caribbean Gothicism.

Caribbean Gothic Writing

Since the early 19th century, the colonial Caribbean has been projected as a place that is associated with terror, whether from the brutality of the colonial system or travelogues, it was shown as either backward, or at times a savage environment. Additionally, early colonial writers presented the place with elements of Gothicism that projected an image of terror, and debauched lifestyles that are enmeshed in the black arts, e.g., obeah, witchcraft, and black magic, as the backdrop of violence.

However, the emergence of a literary tradition in the late 19th century, with Gothicism as a genre, was introduced in Caribbean writings, with writers imitating European linguistic devices and parodying their literary conventions. This style can be seen in the writings of the late 19th and early 20th century, evidencing the emergence of Caribbean Gothic as a genre. These highlighted an interplay of relations between the European **coloniser**, with his tropes of violence, brutality, and atrocities against humans, during slavery, and counter-played by the **colonised,** whose experiences became the subject that characterised Gothicism. A century prior to this period, the tales of the *Tacky Rebellion* in 1760,[8] had presented evidence of gothic tales of atrocities, seen in the brutal slave rebellion against white planters in Jamaica. Arguably, it is said to be one of the first gothic tales from the (English-speaking), or Anglophone Caribbean region.

Then 30 years later, the tale of the brutal destruction and atrocities that destroyed the colony of Saint Domingue, now Haiti, can also be seen as a Caribbean gothic. Similarities are also shown in Joan Dayan's ***Haiti, History, and the Gods*** (1977)[9], which explores the narrative of the Haitian Revolution as a Caribbean gothic tale of colonial horrors, counteracted by the colonised; in ways that project the Caribbean landscape as terrifying.

Today, in the 21st century, a more palatable imagery in the 20th and 21st centuries has been projected by writers and film-makers alike, who present the modern Caribbean landscape as exotically mysterious; a place where piracy once reigned supreme, and projected largely for entertainment in films e.g., Walt Disney's *Pirates of the Caribbean* series[10] and showcased as a preferred destination for holiday-makers seeking *'paradise,'* for their ultimate tourist experience. Such imagery project miles of sun-drenched beaches, tantalizing activities to be found in the oceans, luscious landscapes, atmospheres of cultural music and dancing, fun-filled entertainment, excesses of food and drinks; packaged as the epitome of happiness.

However, in order to explore the Caribbean gothic, one has to begin with characteristic features of Caribbean literatures. They are, at first, intrinsically linked to the tensions between the socio-economic, political, and psychological bond between the master/colonial and the slave/colonised. The result is brutality, which characterised the maintenance of the slave system; one that culminated in untold suffering, deaths, destruction, violence, rape, and mutilation. Therefore, in attempting to come to terms with the foregoing, Caribbean gothic writing has focused on projecting these experiences, by utilising the prevailing belief systems; which were originally based on African religious and cultural traditions. Writers have therefore encapsulated such practices and beliefs in the supernatural, magic, sorcery, voodoo or obeah (which is the use of herbal and animal medicines for healing, rituals; casting of spells; incantations, as coping strategies, as well as a form of threat to their brutal reality; in order to capture their audiences' imagination. The fact is, such practices were outlawed by British colonials in the Caribbean since the 17th century, and this intensified the taboo against their use and perpetuated the aura of mystery in their efficacy. The colonial administration had regarded such practices as having the potential to instigate retaliation; fearful that Obeah or Voodoo leaders could use their influence or powers to incite rebellion against them.

Such fears were not unfounded because Edward Long in reporting on the Tacky Rebellion in his [11]*History of Jamaica* (1774), remarked on the "Coromantyns," who were slaves shipped from the Gold Coast and the *"obeiah-men,"* who he says were the *"Chief oracles"* behind uprisings, influenced others with *"fetish or oath"* to rebel against their masters. This type of practice was confirmed in a Report to the Lords of 1789,[12] which stated that rebellion was influenced by *"Professors of that art"* (meaning Obeah men), who *"gave them powder with which to rub themselves."* This salient trope, used in the Cuban writer, Alejo Carpentier's novel, [13]*The Kingdom of this World* (1949), evidences such forms of Gothicism.

Arguably, Herbert De Lisser's [14]*The White Witch of Rosehall* (1929), is perhaps the most gothic of Caribbean literature. De Lisser introduces a number of gothic characteristics in his text – a plantation Great House, as a haunted space, as well as a number of gothic elements, ranging from necromancy, spells, spirit possession, grave robbery, brutality, seduction, lust, debauchery, white patriarchal sexual politics, and subsequent reign of terror, to criticising the morally corrupt influence of British colonialism in Jamaica/The West Indies.

Unlike De Lisser's Jamaican setting in his *novel*, **The Phantom of the Great House** is a Gothic *play*, set in Grenada, with a sub-genre categorised as, a psychological thriller, (approximately nine decades after De Lisser's novel, and 5 decades after Jean Rhys' *Wide Sargasso Sea* 1966, and Derek Walcott's *Ti-Jean and His Brothers* 1958). This Play is based on the iconic *Great House*, a story from [15]*The New Folktales & Legends for the 21st Century (2018)*, that combines the elements of horror, romance, mystery, seduction, murder, suspense, debauchery, lust, obeah, brutality, zombies, love/lust, treachery, the role of the incubus, madness, the morally corrupt white Planter, and the Great House, as a haunted space.

In this play however, the fearful *Phantom* is presented on several levels. It is a psychic fear, revealed from secrets which unravel through the reminiscences of the following: the two old women, who are past employees of the now abandoned *Great House*; the characters who form the *Chorus* in the play; the experiences of Little Chris and Stella, the Protagonist, during her visit to the Great House in Carriere Estate, Grenada. From these 'witnesses,' psychic fear is explored from different perspectives:

1. It is the subliminal horrors and dangers of the Caribbean physical landscape, experienced by the main characters, Stella, and Christopher. As the younger generation, they debunk myths and concerns about folktales and the supernatural, so have to learn by their mistakes.

2. Psychic fear is real and haunting among those who witnessed the past incidents in the *Great House* and are sworn to keep the information secret, *'till they die'*.

3. Psychic fear is presented as prevalent island-wide, operating socially and culturally, as a belief system, for those who

accommodate the folk culture and folktales of the place. These in turn help to perpetuate fear among the folks, that at least, satisfy the desire to give meaning to the tales' existence, as they are repeated across the generations.

4. Psychic fear is also linked to the history of the island. A history that haunts its people, having left an open chasm of intriguing features, especially the notion of *power*, for disseminating colonisation and its legacy; via the cathartic power of storytelling. Anxieties aroused by colonisation woven into the fabric of Caribbean folk culture in post-slavery, post-colonial Caribbean, are presented as ideological struggles about the representation of power, race, gender, and fear; which are articulated by the folks.

The Play invokes fear created by post-colonial reality, as it was practised by Colonial Planters and dramatizes the power they wielded, which instilled fear among the colonised natives. The *Great House* therefore stands as a symbolic representation or vestige of that power, whose owners, though absent, still seem to 'survive' as fear, in the lives of the people, and also within the environment. It echoes a reversal of cultural anxieties of white races that can be seen as rewriting Mary Shelley's creature,[16] which was coloured partly black, now projected in *A Phantom of the Great House* as a white devil, seen in the character of Mr. McDonald, and the memory of his past activities and power, which still haunts and instils fear in the lives of the locals, (Act 3 Sc 2).

The conversation between *Anancy, Papa Bois, Cricket, Frog and Fire-fly* (Act I Sc I), explores how some of the cultural tales that are least understood, are appropriated as Gothicism within the folktales. These are used to explore meaning behind the standard tropes of the tales, as ideological struggles by the folks themselves, in addressing the sense of fear or representations of horror in their landscape. The tale of the zombie woman, *Mama La Diablese*[17] or visiting Madam Lola, the Obeah woman, and the disappearing ghost or Duppy of Christopher or indeed the threat of fearful consequences associated with these; exist among the locals. They contribute to the post-colonial space; the locus of zombie tales which are necessary for the Caribbean gothic play. This space is contradictory, interwoven with what is both familiar and unfamiliar, and as a result, causes disquiet among relationships in the landscape.

The play also presents another thematic concern - decline of the planter-class in the Caribbean; the fact that the McDonalds' asset, (The *Great House* and its Estate), lay for a decade, deteriorating and dilapidated and is the subject of a land-grab by the government. This situation, minus its patriarchal power, is being passed on to the *mulatto* Stella. Her story examines the decline of the planter-class of Carriere Estate, from her high-brow bourgeois family, played out against the backdrop of a relic of defunct economic and social power. This may suggest that ultimately, the female inheritor is left without powerful patriarchal backing and must, single-handedly, make decisions regarding her own future position. However, Little Chris' setting of the *Great House* on fire, at the end of the Play, could be seen as defiance against Stella's participation as a female, in the representation of corruption, exploitation, and the marred legacy of her colonial icon, in this post-colonial setting. Additionally, his action could suggest that though the ghosts of colonialism and its legacy of psychic fear still haunt the lives of the folks today, taking individual action to rid himself and the island of the 'past', can probably exorcise them, in ways that probably lessen their negative effects on the future.

However, Little Chris is a psychologically complex character, whose life embodies gothic characteristics. He is a tragic figure – cunning and impulsive, with misplaced passion. His flaws are displayed in words, thoughts, and deeds; all which bring about his tragic downfall at the end. He meets the newly arrived Stella, learns of her inherited fortunes, attempts to orchestrate a potential love relationship with her, and sees her as his financial means to his migration from the island to America. Immediately, he uses sorcery to pursue her, and all his actions are done at breakneck speed, until he learns, (when its already too late), that Stella is his sister. His impetuous presumptions with no expression of romantic love, highlights the rapid actions he undertakes, with little or no time-gap between any of the interactions between him, Mama Lola, and Stella. Therefore, his impetuosity contributes to his tragic downfall. Little Chris's misplaced passion is shown at the end of the play (Act 5 Sc 2), when he becomes hysterical and grovels on the ground, weeping and blubbering like a mad man, before eventually committing suicide; by running into the towering inferno that is the *Great House*. He therefore can be seen as sharing the tragic flaw of rashness with [18]Oedipus, exhibited in defiance of Mama Lola's will. When he verbally clashes with her and threatens to return to collect his money, (given to Mama Lola for obeah mischief against Stella), intimating possible violence (Act 5 Sc 1); it is already too late for him to retreat from his course of action. Hoping Mama Lola would capitulate, shows how Little Chris' naivety had blinded him to the reality that he too, could become a victim of her obeah practices.

Therefore, his downfall is a culmination of greed, naivety, manipulation, trickery, and abuse; which perhaps indicates an underlying didacticism or kind of moral punishment for his misdeeds. However, the doctrine of individual responsibility and the post-colonised self, as a social nemesis, suggest different motivations for Little Chris's tragic end. From one perspective, he has become a victim of evil impulses which control his life, from the superstitious world of the obeah woman.[19] On the other hand, in so far as Little Chris is responsible for his own actions, his hamartia and impetuosity bring out a flaw in his character, which is based on excessively striving to use Stella to benefit his personal, financial ambition to exit the island. In other words, his attempted monetary domination is [20]Machiavellian; a trait that made him a slave to his ambitions.

There are other gothic concerns within the Play that link the decline of the planter-class and their behaviour which attempts to shed light on the McDonalds' 'fall from grace' in the environment. Mr. McDonald's denunciation of his wife miscegenation, stems from his belief that her involvement with a native lover usurps his view of the *"natural order"* i.e., the white male dominates the women in his environment (both black and white), for his benefit, and exclusive prerogative. However, once this view is shattered, it turns him into a Gothic villain, whose twisted mind gravitates to using assassins to execute his bestial desires. Consequently, he orchestrates the violent death of his wife's lover, and orders the murder of her illegitimate child, at birth. These are suggestive of several factors relating to the destabilisation of his balance of power:

1. He fears the mixed-race foetus being carried by his wife, would present an unacceptable permanent racial/visual reminder of her infidelity.

2. The exposure of being haunted by guilt of his own infidelity, counterbalanced by his wife's infidelity, resulted in his cuckolded situation.

3. His resultant rage stems also from the embarrassment of being a *Don Juan* himself, who has to live with being secretly judged or jeered by everyone - household staff, friends, and the wider islanders.

4. Additionally, his warning and stringent order of secrecy, to the two Senior Maids in the *Great House*, was aimed at silencing any vulgarity associated with Mrs McDonald's *"whiteness,"* and the black-white love triangle; which is at the centre of the plot.

5. As a result, he becomes a pseudo-masochist, whose erotic behaviour brings him down. Ordering the death of Mrs McDonald's baby at birth reverberates in the play as an attempt to de-eroticise her experiences. He reinforces this by forcing her to discard what he regards as a threat to his masculine power as a Planter, white, and privileged: her black child.

The play is also a narrative of physical and psychological trauma. From a Caribbean cultural perspective, it projects the frightful *"other"* as the white Planter; identifying *"otherness"* as visible by the reader, not from a conventional standpoint but from the other side of the colonial divide. In other words, there is a reversal of the notion of *"otherness,"* predominantly seen in texts *Jane Eyre*,[21] as the *"black, mad or exotic"* character, belonging to a minority cultural group; to one that projects the white planters' *"otherness,"* in the tensions that reverberate across this Caribbean Gothic landscape. Even Stella, through her inheritance of "whiteness" from her undisputed planter hegemony via Mrs. MacDonald, makes her literally, the inheritor of the *Great House*, is also a victim of this thought.

Consequently, when Stella falls down the hole in the landscape surrounding the *Great House*, metaphorically, she also *"falls from grace,"* (similar to her white mother). On a symbolic level, she begins a precipitous downward spiral into unfaithfulness, erotic desires, being hexed, betrayed, and abused by an incubus, (presented as Little Chris), haunted by zombies, inherits an illegitimate pregnancy; are all emphasised in the text, as inherent traits that leads to a similar fate and demise, as her mother. Stella also becomes mad at the end of the play, but unlike her mother, chooses to live, in a way that suggests continuation of the Phantom's legacy; since *Little Chrissy,* the seed of an incubus or Phantom will survive, and possibly inherit the *Great House* in the future!

Zombification

The Play explores *Mama La Diablese, Christopher* and a *Phantom* or [22]*Duppy*, as zombies. These are presented similar to Western gothic genres (in both films and texts); of a murdering creature which terrorises a community and induces dread and fear of their supernatural powers. However, it also possible to view the zombies, as symbolical of a living dead: who are soul-less wanderers, with no prospect of a future path to freedom, appearing to be lost in a wilderness, alienated and feared by all, bent on revenge for past hurt and for being cyclically trapped in a perpetual impasse.

On one level, it is possible to interpret zombification as the process of colonisation on the individual. In other words, the condition of zombification that has robbed the folks of their souls, identity, and the ability to act on their own volition or determine their own futures. Alienated from their original homeland, they inherit a place which could be regarded as a wilderness, and their nomadic existence seen as a search, for restorative paths to freedom. This may take the form of political independence from the coloniser's grasp, or on a personal level, seen as refusing to be suppressed, in what can be seen as a stagnant environment that causes its younger generation to leave the island, to seek betterment abroad, as articulated by Little Chris (Act 2 Sc 2).

Therefore, the existence of *Mama La Diablese, Christopher* and the *Phantom* zombies could be seen as metaphorically exemplifying the strangle-hold or lasting effects of colonial systems and slavery on the psyche of the folks. The fact is, 500 years later, in their post-colonial period, they are still trying to uncover, as well as redirect their history, in ways that enable them to interrogate the vestiges of colonial influences that are still in their lives. This is echoed in the conversations between the members of the **Chorus** in Act 5 Sc 3, in the play.

On another level, the colonial stranglehold can also be seen in Stella's quest, on the micro/personal level, which is linked to what took place on the macro/public level (colonisation) in society. Consequently, the discussions enable an understanding of the island's socio-economic, political, and historical struggles, at the hands of the white Planter-class (past and present), **vis-à-vis** inheritance of the situations the natives find themselves in. Christopher's death in the fire of the *Great House* can be interpreted as negative, where in taking his own life, his action goes beyond the boundaries of gender, race, and island. On a symbolical level, such self-destruction can be interpreted as personification of an entire spectrum of traumatized *Others* within the society. Seen from another perspective, it is regaining the power to make choices, as Stella does at the end of the Play, and could be seen as an attempt to rewrite a different history, as intimated by the **Chorus** in Act 5 Sc 3; from the other side of the colonial divide.

The *Great House* in the Caribbean

There are many examples of the iconic *Great Houses* around the Caribbean. These houses of grandeur were owned and built by Plantation owners during the 15th and 16th centuries, in the height of the Slave Trade and plantation expansion in the region. They were the exclusive residents of the Plantation Sugar Barons. These luxurious mansions ensured their comfortable lifestyles and protection on the Plantations, whilst they conducted their trade of sugar, cocoa, and later bananas in the Caribbean.

These houses varied in content, but their distinctive exclusive designs and styles set them apart from their surroundings. The buildings were large and imposing, consisting, in some cases, of more than 10 bedrooms, a living room, and a dining room surrounded by spacious lobbies. There were upper floors which were accessed via stairs to a landing, with white balustrades, upper story rooms, and often surrounded by more lobbies.

The imposing size and height of these *Great Houses* meant they were often overlooked much of the sugar plantation estates, with uninterrupted views of the Caribbean Sea. In fact, some *Great Houses* were adopted as forts, with 3 feet thick walls, to protect the Sugar Barons, their families, and their flourishing trade. In some cases, security was further strengthened with British troops stationed at all four corners to protect their assets - slave workers and plantations alike. Many were built with glass louver windows and cooler boxes. These mansions had high ceilings, polished wooden floors, and wide verandas, high ceilings and windows that were skilfully constructed from native hardwood.

Additionally, there was the sugar works, which included the sugar mill, boiling house and curing house, offices for the white overseers and clerks, who kept the plantation records, and storing for the processed sugar as well as rum. There were also trash houses for the dried cane, called *bagasse*, which was used as fuel in the boiling houses and stables; (with grooms who kept saddle horses for the masters and mistresses to ride), for the animals. Some Great houses even had hospitals, called "hothouses." Added to these *Great Houses* were specially attached out-buildings, which consisted of storage sheds, household servant's quarters, two kitchens (one for the *Great House* and one for the servants), and a bar, where the owner would entertain his male friends. Some *Great Houses* still exist on several Caribbean islands today.

Significance of the Great House in the Play

Visually, the *Great House,* as a physic entity in the colonised Caribbean landscape, signifies different meanings to each side of the cultural spectrum; reflects Stuart Hall's [23]*Cultural Representation* and the idea of 'shared meanings.' To the white Planter-class, it represents supremacy and the economic wherewithal to oppress others. To the black natives, it instils deep-seated subjugated posturing, and a wider cultural message of fear of what is unknown about the place and those who operate it. Therefore, a racialised discourse is presented by binary oppositions as follows:

1. The white race has intellectual development, refinement, learning and knowledge, represented by the construction of a unique building, (appearing as an institution), seemingly formalised, with an air of "civilised restraint," that gives the impression of a high culture within.

2. On the other hand, the link between the black natives' perceived lack of civilised refinement, their reliance on local, traditional customs and rituals, and their lack of competitive civil institutions; create polarised stereotyping on both sides. As a result, there is a general mystique surrounding the *Great House,* which gives the impression of secrecy in its activities. Consequently, those who live within its structure, are presented as impressive, and at times, baffling to outsiders.

There are two key terms to consider here; *"great"* and *"house,"* and within this consideration, other words, such as, *"context"* and *"object,"* are immediately highlighted, to reflect how as an *object*, the *Great House* acquires meaning, within the historical *context* of its location. The etymology of the word "great" is Old English of West Germanic origin, *"grauta"* related to Dutch *"groot"* and Saxon *"grot"*. It means "big," "tall," "thick," "stout," "massive." It's Latin root word, *"magn"* means "great," also includes "magnificent," "magnitude" and "magnanimous." Therefore, the physicality of the *Great House* is meant to instil a promise of stability, greatness, eminence and suggests the unique structure belongs to a world that is set apart from the mundane/natives. However, the idea that the physical building exists, marking a historical time period, opens certain doors of meaning on the symbolical, as well as cultural levels, in its immediate environment.

The fact is, the *Great House* as a historically constituted space, represents an ideology that is linked to British colonisation. On one hand, in the Caribbean environment, it functions as a purposeful mixture of British imperialism and dominance. On the other hand, it functions on the level of myth, because it embodies a chain of causes and effects, linked to oppression. These are characterised by suffering, via violence, brutality, atrocities against the human spirit, death, mystery, and actions within its mystical or gothic space; made possible by an established hierarchy. In other words, the building, known as the *Great House*, is a radical historicized concept of power, through its interplay of relations. It also highlights the question of *class*-power and *class*-interests, by repressing what it seeks to control; the native people who work within and for it. Therefore, the idea of mysticism it invites, lends itself to construction of various 'outsider' narratives; based on their own perception of what occurs within that space, and interpretation, as per their own belief-systems.

Language Issues – The Polylingual Environment

The issues of language used by the Caribbean writer in presenting his writing, is a long debated one; stemming largely from the 1930's emergence of a Caribbean written tradition. The dilemma faced by the early writers, which is relatable today, centres on the pros and cons of using Standard English, or non-Standard forms e.g., dialect, and Creolised forms of speech to present their work. Early Caribbean writing shows that an individual writer's choice of medium was based on their targeted audiences, therefore Standard English was used. Reasons proffered were that using the non-standard English forms meant that the work would be limited to a parochial audience, despite their greater understanding of the Creole language varieties.

Therefore, the choice of using Standard English, to gain a wider audience, meant losing the "authenticity" of voices and speech varieties that aid meaning in context, within the text. This is because the written Standard English form tended not to fully represent the "voice" of the folks. Added to this dilemma was the fact that publishers of Caribbean writings, were based outside of the Caribbean, e.g., London and USA, and their decisions to publish a writer's work, influenced by strict adherence to Western conventional writing forms, meant they imposed restrictions on the non-Standard forms being used. Either way, the Caribbean writers' constriction meant that they were not "free" to write as they pleased. However, since the mid-20th century, though writers have overcome much of the earlier restrictions, some are still faced with the dilemma of whether to maintain characteristic features of the Creolised spoken varieties, to convey a sense of Caribbean identity within the canon; (since it enables some representation of nuances, and localised meanings); whilst others choose to modify the language, in order to appeal to both Standard English and non-Standard English speakers alike.

What is undisputed, is that the Caribbean does have a polylingual environment which stems from its racially mixed background. This is due to slavery and colonisation, by a mixture of English, Dutch, French, and Spanish settlers, who were white, and to a much larger extent, West African slaves, indentured Indian labourers, and much later, other settlers. Slaves, being the larger percentage of the population, came predominantly from three West African areas: in the 17th century from Senegal to Sierra Leone, from Liberia to Nigeria in the 18th century and in the last period of slavery from Angola. Each African area consisted of their own tribal groups. The British colonial administration consisted of people from different parts of the UK, i.e., Scotland, Wales, or Ireland, and each with their own brand of colloquial and regional dialects. Added to this linguistically mixed situation in 1800, were the indigenous Amerindian languages, which created a fusion or synthesis of languages in the Caribbean environment. Therefore, far from being one Caribbean language, there were several permutations of speech that created what is recognised as a **Creole language**. A Creole language is identified by its combination of African syntax and European lexicon/words. This development of the Creole language was confirmed by [24]J.J. Thomas, who identified the Creole language as *"a dialect framed by Africans from a European tongue."*

    Today, although there is an acknowledgement of Standard English, as the official form of communication, in most English-speaking Caribbean islands, there are islands whose history evidence exchanges of European domination, so that one island may have more than one Western language spoken in its environment. This is demonstrated throughout this Play, being a Grenadian environment, which inherited a French-based language, as well an English based language; fused in the island over time, with other varieties as already stated, produced its unique style of speaking and writing; resulted in both **English Creole** and **French Creole** languages.

    However, the French-based language has had less officially enforced means of communication, compared to the British Standard English; due to the shorter time the French colonials ruled Grenada. Notwithstanding this, vestiges of French Creole are still used by the older generation; represented by the **Chorus** in the Play. They are also identified in some utterances among the older folks, regarded as a "dying" language which is stylized, but is becoming an anomaly in the modern environment. So, when Ruth says to Daisy, [25]*Sese Mwen, ca c'est comess, oui!* (Act 2 Sc 5), she is drawing fully on the past French colonial influence in Grenada's linguistic background. More specifically, in this Play, the resulting

INTRODUCTION   xxv

Creole French speech patterns, are still used by the old women, Daisy and Ruth, who are both over 80 years old. This is because the younger generations, have not made it a part of their everyday discourse, for many reasons. Therefore, translation is often sought, for an understanding of their meanings. One of the main concerns voiced within the Play, (Act 2 Sc 5), is based on the erosion of such language, and accompanying cultural traditions facing extinction; though this is impacted on by several factors.

These factors relate to the changing ways of life, influenced by globalisation, as well as other *external* factors; such as migration to metropolitan cities, and the necessity of Standard English usage for all official communication – media platforms, legal institutions, and education. Added to these are *internal* factors, which have influenced the language of the people, such as migration within the islands of the Caribbean region. The latter has resulted in strong similarities in vocabulary, syntax, and morphology, between Caribbean islands. In the *Phantom of the Great House*, the character *Papa Bois*, as the name implies, has its origin in French. It means (*Father of the woods*) in French, suggesting that in the Caribbean, this folkloric icon in the play, may have stemmed from French-Creole speakers i.e., Africans and French colonists, who settled in the island; Grenada being a French colony between 1694 – 1763.

Language Issues – Characteristic Features of the Creole Language

It is important to note that orthography (spelling) of the Creole languages varies greatly, within Caribbean islands, since some choose to spell them phonetically e.g., *cyan,* for (can't); *kudnt,* for (couldn't); *whey* for (where), *mi* for *me*, and *seh* for *say*. The variety of Creolised spelling is most noticeable from island to island in the proverbial sayings. As far as this *Phantom of the Great House* is concerned, the importance attached to the Creole language, is Its marked difference from Standard English. This is highlighted to draw attention to aspects of the language in the island/region, and the concern for their increasing departure from some cultural expressions. These are use of Proverbial expressions among the younger generation, and their lack of up-take among them, from

INTRODUCTION   xxvi

the older generation. As with the concern for the waning traditional customs and activities, articulated by the **Chorus**, a similar concern for the language is also intimated, since language is inextricably tied up with traditional expressive forms.

Here are some characteristic features of the **Creole language** used within this Play.

1. There is **no nasalisation at the end of words**, particularly when it's used to present participle of verbs e.g., *going, worrying, helping, liming*: Instead, these are used: *goin', worryin', helpin' limin',* (Act 1 Sc 1), (Act 2 Sc 5), (Act 3 Sc 4), Act 5 Sc 3).

2. **Creole English does not have the [nt] cluster** at the end of negative contracted forms, such as *can't, don't couldn't.* Instead, these forms are used: *cyan, doh,* (Act 4 Sc 3) e.g. *"Papa Gawd, you cyan do this to me!"*

3. The **dental aspirate is omitted in words** such as: *the, this, them, they, that.* Instead, these forms are used: *de, dis, dey, dem* and *dat,* e.g. *"But dey say he didn' mean for them to kill Christopher."* (Act 3 Sc 4).

4. The common **use of the first pronoun I, which is often replaced by *ah*,** or used interchangeably, to create emphasis in speech, based on emotions being presented. For example, the sentence, *I don't know*, is presented as *"Ah doh know."* (Act 1 Sc 1).

5. **Word order is often reversed**, so that instead of saying *all of you*, is presented as *"all-you."* (Act 1 Sc 1).

6. **Omission of verbs** is common in **Creole English**, so that instead of *"Lots of them up in your area?"* Instead of, *"Are there lots of them in your area?"* In Act 2 Sc 5, Anancy says, *"And if we not careful, soon people go laugh at our stories."*

7. In most cases, Creole English **omits the third person singular** (s) at the end of verbs. Example: *"He plan to*

marry her." Instead of, "He plans to marry her." Or (Act 2 Sc 5), "It's because no one going to see us in all this light."

8. **Repetition is used to convey emphasis or a sense of immediacy.** For example, in Act 3 Sc 2, Ruth tells Daisy, "Is glad ah glad to see you." (Act 1 Sc 1), "Well is come she comin'," and "Well is wayward they wayward both of them." (Act 4 Sc 3).

9. **Different uses of pronouns to reflect Creolised pattern of speech** e.g. mi = me; dem = them. "Ah got t'ings off mi chest." (Act 4 Sc 3).

10. Use of **double negatives** e.g. "I don't want no trouble today, eh!" (Act2 Sc 3).

11. **Omission of past tense verbs** e.g. "So ah quickly shapeshift into a wild boar." (Act 1 Sc 1).

12. A noticeable feature of the island's linguistic background is the **language fusion** that has taken place in Grenada. This has resulted in both **French-based** and **English-based Creole varieties.** Both are referred to as *patois*, pronounced *pat-wa*, e.g., **French patois** or **English patois** with the following features:
    (a) A sentence can begin in one language and end with another,
    (b) A sentence can be purely French-based or English-based
    (c) A sentence can have a mixture of both languages in the same sentence.

For example:
1. *Sese mwen, that is comess!* (A mixture of both **French Creole and Standard English**), (Act 2 Sc 5).
2. *Comme si, comme ca* (**French**), (Act 2 Sc 5).
3. *Papa mwen, ça c'est comess, oui!* (**French Creole and French**), Act 2 Sc 5.
4. *Ah go tell them about me French background, oui!* (Begins with **Creolised English** and ends with **a single French word**), (Act 5 Sc 3).

It is important to note that Caribbean writers present the Creolised languages as they are expressed in their individual environments. For example, islands such as Martinique, Guadeloupe, Grenada, and Dominica, where French colonials dominated or still do today, speak French, as an official language *(Martinique and Guadeloupe are still French colonies).* However, in Grenada's case, there are vestiges of the French language, uttered mostly among the older generation. However, attempts have been made to create a regional orthography, as seen in the various editions of [26]Richard Allsopp's *Dictionary of Caribbean English Usage*. In addition, there are other suggested standards of orthography and pronunciation across various islands; all which attest to a movement away from the strictures of the inherited Standard Western forms of language and speech. Such movements are attempts to give primacy to the localised versions of Caribbean speech, as well as individual language identities within the region. The flourish of individual island language dictionaries, now accessible globally, also evidence this growing phenomenon.[27] However, in *The Phantom of the Great House*, despite the characteristic features of Creole languages presented, there is also an attempt to modify the presentation of both the Creole and Standard English formations used. Strategies included in this Play are as follows:

1. Adapting some of the Creole forms, especially omitting the *"g"* in present continuous verb tenses, such as, *goin',* and other characteristic features, as outlined above. These are presented in the language of the **Chorus**, who symbolically present the speech of the older generation.

2. Choosing to maintain some of the Standard English forms, to make it easily accessible to purely Standard English readers, especially students.

3. Characters revert to Creole English, as the natural vernacular, especially when displaying emotions.

4. Making subtle distinctions in the varieties of language used, between older generation characters and the

INTRODUCTION   xxix

younger Caribbean speakers. For example, allowing for the formally educated characters to use a greater content of Standard English e.g., Christopher, than those without formal schooling e.g., Ruth and Daisy; whose patterns of speech include more Creole varieties, (both French- and English-based).

These strategies have been used to ensure that a middle-ground is achieved, so as not to limit its global reach, or identification as a Caribbean Gothic Play, but firmly establish its existence within the Caribbean canon.

Language Issues - Proverbial Sayings

> *"The Caribbean proverb is the weaponised discourse*
> *of sophisticated elders, deployed with efficacy,*
> *to force the younger generations to hunt for the*
> *bullet and return to the source, from where it was fired!"*
> R. Thompson

The Phantom of the Great House is framed by Acts and Scenes which are structured to reflect the sentiments of the **Proverbial Sayings** that preface them; in order to highlight important issues presented within them. The concerns of the changing landscape, socially, politically, economically, and culturally, are voiced by the characters who make up the **Chorus**. As such, symbolically, they represent a generation in limbo, located in the middle of two phases: since they have experienced life with the aging population and are witnessing the present apathy for traditional customs, among the younger generation; that raise concerns about proverbs' future survival on the island.

The **Chorus** presents the Play's main concerns as a *lament*, but at the same time, are aware that they too, must adapt to changes in a modern world; to benefit from the encroaching globalised factors that *'push'* and *'pull'* their younger generations away from the island; especially from embracing the island's traditional values and landscape, as viable options to remain. Overall, such wisdom is expressed within the proverbs, to suggest a re-examination of the

INTRODUCTION

old customs, to gain knowledge from past lessons, in order to redirect society.

Originally, proverbs in the Caribbean were an integral part of the culturally mixed environment and passed on from generation to generation for hundreds of years. Although used mainly by the older generation, to the younger, they are still in some use today, as part of the everyday speech among senior citizens. Proverbs are famous for their peculiar elegance, brevity of wit, or their encapsulation of wisdom.

A proverb or proverbial phrase is a type of expression, transmitted via Caribbean oral traditions, that is usually instructive, and used to illustrate ideas or reinforce arguments; overall, it is used to deliver an important message. This message could be to console, caution, advise, defend, inspire, or reinforce an argument.

The Caribbean region has inherited most of its proverbs from a mixture of sources, mainly due to its multiracial background. According to conventional etiquette, the proverb is uttered by an older to a younger person, since the passing on of wisdom, constitutes a respect for the experiences and accumulation of knowledge gained by elders, from having lived longer than a young person. Young people are therefore expected to embrace them with respect and unquestionable acceptance. The fact is, it is considered unconventional or disrespectful, for young people to use proverbs to an older person; suggestive of claiming to be wiser than an elder.

Used in this Play, their utterances are among the older generation, as a natural response to various situations. This demonstrates that the Caribbean culture's richness in them, among the older generation, is still a very effective strategy, in ensuring the efficacy of meaning in speech. However, the use of the proverb, as a cultural and linguistic expression, (as with some of the other cultural traditions intimated among the **Chorus**), appear to be also disappearing.

The point being made is that the younger generation, the educated elite, and the general population seem to have lost their competent use of proverbs in everyday speech; preferring to see them as historical utterances, that make their presence in Caribbean language seem peculiar. The dominant perception is that it is just the language of the *old folks*; meaning *older generation*, therefore suggesting it is not meritorious in a modern context. Furthermore, the dominance of Standard English, used in all modes of communication and on all formal platforms, make the use of proverbs, seem anachronistic, relegated to the past, uttered in domestic situations, and referred to as what, ***"they say,"*** (in Jamaican patois, ***"Weh dem seh"");*** generally referring to the *old folks*.

Such evaluations can be interpreted from two perspectives: The expression, ***"They say,"*** give authority to, and acknowledge the wisdom expressed in the proverbs by the *old folks* or *older generation*. The fact that the plural pronoun, ***"they"*** is used in a generic way, signifies the **collective wisdom** of the folks, which give proverbs a certain efficacy of authority in communication. (Act 3 Sc 4).

At the same time, these proverbs are less used because of their relegation to the periphery of popular discourse, and result in having to understand their values and meaning via translations. It can be seen that instead of shoring up their aesthetic and educational values in official communicative language, and frequent usage, the majority of references to Caribbean proverbs are either defined as *"slang", "sayings", "expressions," "things granny used to say," "popular sayings,"* or *"quotes."* This means they are viewed as uncouth, or as one media platform defines them, *"sayings that have been passed down through the generations are quirky, informative and sometimes downright hilarious."*[28] In other words, suggesting proverbs have an anomalous relationship with the Standard forms or official languages used.

Notwithstanding the *old vs young* linguistic dichotomy, the Caribbean proverb is the weaponised discourse of sophisticated elders, deployed with efficacy, to force the younger generations to hunt for the bullet, and return to the source from where it was fired! In other words, the historicity of these utterances and the value they bring to understanding Caribbean speech patterns and usage, highlight the importance of their source! Therefore, returning to the source, is key to gaining holistic insight about the Caribbean, its people's discourse, and their thought-processes. It is one of the reasons why Caribbean proverbs are prominent in *Phantom of the Great House*; as a means of recapturing the former spirituality of the folks.

In the Play, their inclusion show that such expressions have several origins, based on the socio-economic, historical, political, and cultural synthesis, that have taken place in the Caribbean region, over the past five centuries. One reason for this is that Proverbs operate as historical markers, by their distinctive language input, (e.g., *French-based, African-based, or English-based*, etc), and highlight the interferences from colonisation that produced a mixture of orthography, linguistic construction, subject-matter, cultural richness, didacticism, and in some cases, self-contradictions.

Framed in the Acts and Scenes of the play, these proverbs are deployed with efficacy, since they draw attention to both their presence and the weaponised meanings that are adapted for use against adverse or challenging situations, that may require verbal defence, advice, caution, or good sense. Used as Epithets in 9 scenes within the play, they function as follows:

Act 2 Scene 2 – *Young with guts like cobo.*
Cobo is a large carrion feeding bird of prey. Here it is used to **describe** someone who can withstand great pressure and is unmoved by challenges and difficulties. In the Play, it describes Little Chris and Stella's apathy to traditions in general, and the way they are undeterred by rumours of the Great House being haunted or its past history, despite the prevalence of fear of the house and its association, on the island.

Act 2 Scene 4 – *What you head lead you to do, you backside go pay for it!*
This proverb means whatever actions you plan and orchestrate, be aware that you will have to accept the consequences of such actions. This is usually uttered as a **threat or warning** of physical

beating (generally uttered from parents to children). It is similar to; *you reap what you sow*. In the Play, the implication is that in stubbornly going to the haunted house, Stella suffers rape by an incubus, in the form of Christopher, which has lasting consequences for them both.

Act 3 Scene 2 – *Let sleeping dogs lie*.
This proverb is said to **advise** someone that they should not talk about a bad situation that most people have forgotten. In other words, it's best to leave a situation as it is, because disturbing it might stir up trouble again. Daisy and Ruth's apprehension about meeting Stella and having to recall memories they would prefer to 'forget' till they die, is a case in point.

Act 3 Scene 3 – *Fattening Frog for Snake*
This proverb refers to a man who cares for a woman and treats her well, should be **cautious** that his actions won't go to waste by losing her to another man, who will benefit from his good deeds. Here, the reference is to Little Chris' attitude and actions of attempting to capture Stella with a love potion, oblivious of the fact that she is already betrothed to Alex, her Fiancé in London.

Act 4 Scene 2 – *Laugh and cry does live in the same house*
There is a **cautionary** suggestion here, that the things which make you happy, could also bring you pain. Mama Lola and her obeah are, interchangeably, a potential threat and danger to Little Chris, despite using them both for his benefit. In other words, the suggestion is, whatever brought him joy, could also bring him pain.

Act 4 Scene 3 – *Doh count egg in fowl bottom*
Similar to, *'Don't count your chickens before they're hatched*. In its **advisory** capacity this proverb suggests that you should not make plans based on things you are not certain of. Little Chris' misconception that his actions to capture Stella and benefit from his obeah-wedding, are a *fait accompli*, until he learns the truth that he is Stella's brother; presents a 'romantic' relationship that is ill-fated from the start.

Act 5 Scene 1 – *Moon run faas till day ketch 'im*
This proverb, **instilling good sense,** means you can't run forever, one day you will face the consequences of your actions or misdeeds. The client-Obeah woman relationship between Mama Lola and Little Chris seemed very good until they clashed; shows how they both face the consequences of their actions – exposure, contention, revenge, and destruction.

Act 5 Scene 2 – *Hang you basket whe you can reach it*
A similar proverb is, *"Don't hang your heart where your hand can't reach."* They both have the same **advisory** meaning: keep your goals within your abilities and means. The result of Little Chris' presumption that he could be *'Master'* of the Great House, if he marries Stella, via deception and cunning, was ill-conceived and certainly not within his grasp, as he had believed.

Act 5 Scene 3 – *When coco ripe it mus' burs'*
The **logic** that this proverb presents is that all will be revealed when the time is right. The revelation of the brother-sister relationship between Stella and Little Chris, the resultant catastrophe brought about by Little Chris' death by burning in the *Great House*; Alex's failure to arrive on the island or Stella's 'loss' of her Fiancé without explanation; Stella's madness; ending up in a mental hospital, where she gives birth to Little Chrissy – all brought matters to a head, in an explosive way that culminated in destruction, death, madness and a questionable future.

Each proverb operates metaphorically, as a loaded gun with bullets, and weaponised meanings, expressed within stylized discourses that make them unique in the cultural tradition. In (Act 4 Sc 1), Ruth, the old maid from the *Great House,* explains the value of proverbial sayings to Stella thus; *"If yuh really study them good; they have wisdom."* Therefore, the general concern in the Play is that a lack of such cultural stabilisers in popular language use, could suggest proverbs are in imminent danger to the culture, of becoming extinct.

INTRODUCTION

> **The Chorus**

One of the main functions of the Chorus in a typical Greek tragedy, where the idea originated, is to create atmosphere and underscore the tragic action. The noun *"chorus"* comes from the Greek word *"khoros"*, via the Latin *"chorus,"* was first used in English in the mid-6th century, for the group of singers and dancers who performed in Greek religious festivals and theatrical performances. However, in *Phantom of the Great House*, the homogenous group forming the **Chorus**; *are Anancy, Cricket, Papa Bois, Firefly, and Frog*. Their individual identities reveal they are Caribbean iconic characters or participants in the Caribbean story-telling tradition, who, having witnessed the folkloric events over generations, command the authority to pass judgement on matters that concern their society. Through their social commentary, they share in the action as individual narrators but also represent the collective voice of the older generation. Although they comment on themes that might suggest how the audience should react to them, they offer insights, background, and summary information, to help the audience follow the performance. In *Phantom of the Great House*, from a stage management perspective, they only narrate, unlike the singing and dancing of the Chorus in a Greek Tragedy.

> **Anancy**

Anancy's significance to the story-telling tradition is embodied in his historical transition from Africa to the Caribbean. He is called Anancy but can be referred to in other islands as *Brer Anancy, Anansi, Ananse or Mrs. Anancy*. This character originated from West Africa, where he was originally an Akan god, who knows and sees everything; an omniscient and omnipotent sky god in the Akan language; considered to be the spirit of all knowledge. When he was brought to the Caribbean by the Slaves, his characteristics altered; he became a trickster figure, whose aim was to help the slaves outwit their slave-master by using cunning. Anancy is a Caribbean icon, whose survival in the Caribbean and his cunning ways symbolise resistance to powerful slave owners and colonisation. In the *Phantom of the Great House,* he is presented as an elder, who passes judgement, based on his wisdom and experiences, to the younger generation and audiences, through his narration. Symbolised as a repository of oral storytelling in the Caribbean environment, he suggests ways society might be redirected, to adapt to the changing landscape, because having existed from the beginning of the 'making of the Caribbean,' he is a reliable witness of the changing nature of society during slavery on plantations, to present day. He is therefore able to bridge the gap between the older and the younger generations, whose apathy to cultural traditions is considered a future risk factor, within the landscape.

> **Papa Bois**

Papa Bois is known as *Maitre Bois*, in areas where Creole is spoken, (St. Lucia, Dominica, Guadeloupe, Grenada, Martinique) and also called *Daddy Bouchon* (hairy man), in other islands. The name is French originated and translated means *(Father of the Woods)*, suggesting that this tale in the Caribbean may have stemmed from French-speaking Africans from the Gold Coast with the input of French colonization in the areas of the Caribbean. In the Caribbean, as was the practice in Africa, *Papa Bois* must be appeased before the forest could be disturbed. Therefore, one has to seek his permission before cutting wood or trees from the forest. Interestingly, this strict rule of taking only what is needed, and nothing more, informs a conservationist and environmentally conscious attitude towards nature, among the African slaves, who brought this tradition to the Caribbean.

The other members of the **Chorus** in the *Phantom of the Great House,* are presented symbolically as, 'Keepers' of the traditional culture, despite their physical form. They are part of the night-time singing insects in the Caribbean, namely; cicadas (the latter mostly daytime till evening), crickets, grasshoppers, and katydids. The latter has a male which produces loud calls whilst searching for a female mate. The sounds produced by these insects may just sound like one long chorus during the night, but each one is unique to its specie.

INTRODUCTION

➢ **Firefly**

An elder with wisdom to comment on society, Firefly can be recognised in the Caribbean because these insects have special luminous organs on their bodies that allow them to flash at nights, during the mating season and storytelling sessions. The flashing is a blinking yellow, orange, or red light, used to attract the opposite sex. Females usually larger than the males, have one lighted segment. Adult fireflies feed on dew droplets, pollen, or nectar from flowers, and some are known to eat smaller insects. Firefly's strategic position in the landscape at night, suggests he represents a credible witness of the events as they unfold.

➢ **Cricket**

Symbolically, an elder, Cricket also has the authority to comment because of his night-time location. As soon as night comes, there is a pervasive, high-pitched kind of metallic buzzing sound made by crickets. Most male crickets make a loud chirping sound at night and during the day they hide in cracks, under bark, inside curling leaves, under stones or fallen logs, or in the cracks in the ground. They are mainly nocturnal, characterised by their *Leep! Leep! Leep!* These sounds are like the persistent ringing of night-time bells, which begin as soon as it is dark, and continue until sunrise. Like the Firefly, they too have a singing specie via tympana on the tibia on their front legs. Being a night-time creature, Cricket has first-hand knowledge of the nightly storytelling tradition.

➢ **Frog**

Frog has earned his right as a symbolic Elder, to pass on wisdom and comment on society, having witnessed generations of the storytelling traditions. The species of whistling frog, native to Grenada, is responsible for the chorus of chirps heard on warm nights or after heavy rain. They are recognised by the male frog's large throat pouch, which inflates and deflates as it whistles. The chorus they create nightly and during storytelling, from the persistent *"Gleep! Gleep!"* are like sleigh bells jingling in the dark.

These *"elders,"* as traditional wisdom dictates in a Caribbean society, (reflecting a mixed racial background, or presented as a microcosm of society), are considered to be dignified and powerful figures; knowledgeable and wise. They are transmitters of culture, guardians of the secrets of life and guides to the young. They are also arbiters of conflicts and preservers of peace amongst members of the community. In other words, their language and wisdom are seen as authentic expressions of the community's experience and reality.

However, in a modern, post-colonial context, with the demands made on the Caribbean economy for rapid growth and expansion, migration to places like England, USA, Canada, and countries in the diaspora, not only resulted in brain- and skills-drainage, but established a concept that a person's general route to improvement and advancement, is to be found in migrating from the islands.

Additionally, migration internally, from predominantly rural areas to urban cities, means that the traditional roles played by the elders: family educators, herbalist, faith encourager, agriculturalists, family chef, babysitters, economists, family mid-wives, rearers of grandchildren, psychologists, and storytellers passing on the culture; no longer ensured that a child would never live alone. The prevailing situation was, whether a child's biological family was present or not, these elders' roles reinforced the concept that, *"it takes a village to bring up a child."* Therefore, the **Chorus'** lament is against their feelings of being less valued, as well as the isolation brought on by modernisation, (education, migration, urbanisation, industrialisation, and the impact of social media), present factors that preclude their participation and continuing involvement in developing the community and nation. Their *lament* could also be seen as a global human right one; an appeal against rising ageism and declining respect for the elderly.

INTRODUCTION

Journey to Self-discovery

Stella's journey, from London to the Caribbean island of Grenada, can be seen as a journey to a discovery of herself. This first began with her inquisitive nature, and determination to interrogate a legacy that was Willed to her, (a *Great House* and its vast Estate). As the only surviving next-of-kin, her mission was to find answers for the psychologically disjointed upbringing, she experienced as a child. The chaotic network of relationships she experienced, made her background seem abstract; living with an aunt, without a mother, with whom they subsequently lost touch during her growing years; learning that the person whom she acknowledged as her biological mother was in fact, a working maid, within the *Great House*, who was betrayed and forced to keep a deplorable secret of fake motherhood throughout her life. This rhizomatic nature of Stella's background, seem to mirror the island's own identity, in a relational context.

Her initial verbal struggles with her Fiancé Alex, in London, at the start of the play, represents her internal conflict of trying to find a way to reconcile the two worlds that she now has a legal affinity to; the Caribbean and London. Therefore, attempting to close the distance between the two worlds, can be seen as a means of healing Stella's personal and cultural past.

Stella's parents (white mother and black father), present a biracial approach to constructing an identity that is interconnected with the passing on of a legacy; albeit, a symbol of corruption, connected to British colonial identity; reflects [29]Edouard Glissant's model of *Relation*. Stella needs to situate herself in a *Relational* network, in order to understand herself, the reason why a legacy has been passed on to her, and its corresponding links to her background. This *Relational* activity is achieved by leaving her Fiancé in England, despite his strong disapproval, and journeying to the Caribbean, in order to establish contact with the physicality and background of the *Great House*, in Grenada.

The quest to bond with the *Great House* as owner, where there was disconnection or a sense of rupture at birth, enables her to experience shared memories from the elderly Maids, who assist in constructing her own identity. Therefore, the nomadic background to her story, as revealed in the discussion with the two women, makes her particularly attuned to the transnational and polyphonic nature of her Caribbean identity. There is no obvious emotional reaction to her established knowledge of a link between her biological mother or her murdered father, but she accepts the legacy willingly; which makes her an ambiguous and emotionally detached individual.

However, Stella was able to construct a portrait of her biological mother and father, via Ruth and Daisy's memories of the *Great House*, woven with fundamental links between her white Planter-class, colonial mother, as well as the Kents who preceded the McDonalds, and her black labourer father; who was brutally assassinated by her step-father. The chaotic network of relationship she inherited, revealed yet another layer of relational and emotional trauma, likened to a fugue; where all the elements of chaos and conflict are revealed. Examples are, the localised amnesia Stella experiences, after being raped whilst unconscious, in the *Great House*; discovery that Chris, the person she had had an intimate relationship with, was in fact her brother; eventual loss of her Fiancé, Alex; all seem to psychologically unhinge Stella. Notwithstanding these, the resultant madness she experiences, seem to mimic an intuitive grasp of reality for her, and may have peculiarly manifested into an epiphany; hence her choice to remain on the island and instal her new type of administration and management via her own structure – a house of freedom.

Benítez-Rojo[30] stresses that such chaos is not necessarily a negative phenomenon; since it also characterises an opportunity for new and beneficial outcomes. Once Stella learns about her background, the play ends with the birth of her illegitimate child, in a mental hospital, which underlines the continuity of tragic possibilities of *Relationship* and its impact on family and social connections. However, it could also reinforce the idea that by deciding to remain on the island and live in the *Great House,* can be seen as a point of transformation in Stella's life; one that will also have consequences for (her son), Little Chrissy in the future.

In other words, from a past of conflicted female relationships *(mother/Aunt Vera/The two maids, Daisy and Ruth, and her 'surrogate' house-maid 'mother')*, Stella's final actions could be interpreted as having released these powerless females from the shackles of subservience, and servitude (especially their burdened life-long secret), to make appropriate self-determined decisions in their lives. Overall, Stella's journey which began as a female embroiled in a complex web of lies, mystery, betrayal, manipulation, violence, and abuse, has culminated with acceptance of her place in Caribbean bourgeois society, as the new or current *"Madam,"* signalling a range of future possibilities.

The conclusion of the Play projects Stella's journey of discovery as a metaphor for acceptance, recovery, and assertion of her female space. Whereas this was once a symbol of alienation – the McDonald's past, the background to her existence, and being three times abandoned by all the men in her life, *(Little Chris, Alex and Christopher, her father)*; this juncture seems to suggest a reconciliation between her past, present, and future. The next stage in her life's journey, as *"Madam"* of the *Freedom House*, suggests matriarchal dominance that could enable construction of a future generation of women, with power and influence on the island.

Roselle Thompson
London 2021

NOTES TO THE INTRODUCTION

1. **Mise-en-abime** (also **mise en abyme**), occurs within a text when there is a duplication or reduplication of images and concepts that refer to the text. As a literary technique, Mise-*en-abîme,* presents subtexts, as well as signifiers within the text, that mirror each other on different levels. In other words, the text presents the frame story or main narrative, from which the reader is taken to other related tales within the text, that repeatedly mirror the main theme and are inextricably linked to it.
2. **Treaty of Paris 1763** - The Treaty of Paris, signed in Paris by representatives of King George III of Great Britain and representatives of the United States of America on September 3, 1783, officially ended the American Revolutionary War.
3. **Treaty of Versailles 1783** was the primary treaty produced by the Paris Peace Conference at the end of World War I. All Germany's overseas colonies in China, in the Pacific, and in Africa were taken over by Britain, France, Japan, and other Allied nations. Germany was stripped of its overseas colonies, its military capabilities were severely restricted, and it was required to pay war reparations to the Allied countries.
4. **Mulatto** or *mulato* in Spanish: A term used to refer to the offspring of a Negro and white European. In the Caribbean this would have been children of slaves and slave masters.
5. **Creole** (noun); a word which originated during the colonial era, is a person of mixed Europeans, (e.g., British, French, Spanish, Dutch) Amerindians and Africans. Used as an adjective, the term is used to refer to the process of creolisation.

6. *Crick-crack storytelling* - These African folktale traditions are well-known and practised within the Caribbean territories. Whilst some may vary in renditions, they are all variants from a common origin. One major characteristic in the storytelling is that it embodies performance. The **'Crick Crack'** storytelling is a group performance in which the 'audience' participates in a close connection between the performer or storyteller and the audience. It presents an African format of a leader or storyteller and a chorus which is the audience, participating in a whole storytelling session.

    In other parts of the Caribbean e.g., St. Lucia, the storytelling is performed in French Creole or Patois and the Leader or Conteur, does a similar announcement that the story is about to be told, by calling out **"Crick!"** ("Kwik" in patois), to which the audience responds by shouting **"Crack!""** or **"Kwak!"** Once the utterance "crick-crack" is completed, the Leader/Conteur continues by testing the audience with riddles, to which they would shout out the answers, in a session of exchanges. After this the story is told. The audience then becomes a chorus that is not only listening but also commenting. Often the riddles and exchanges are about their environment or what is known to them.

7. *Liming* - hanging out/socialising in an informal relaxing environment, especially with friends.

8. **Tacky's Rebellion in 1760** – also called **Tacky's War**, was a slave revolt or uprising from the Akan (Coromanti) slaves that occurred from May to July 1760, in Jamaica. It was one of the most significant slave rebellions in the Caribbean between 1733 and 1791, which included the Slave Insurrection on St. John and the Haitian Revolution.

9. Joan Dayan (1998) ***Haiti, History and the Gods***: University of California Press.

10. *Pirates of the Caribbean* series (2003,2006,2007,2011,2017); a series

of fantasy swashbuckler films produced by Jerry Bruckheimer and based on Walt Disney's theme park attraction of the same name.
11. Long E. (1774): *History of Jamaica*, London, 3 Vols. (London: T. Lowndes. 1774), II 451-52,473.
12. Report to the Lords of the Committee of the Council Appointed for the Consideration of All Matters Relating to Trade &Foreign Plantation (London, 1789).
13. Carpentier A. (1949:2006): T*he Kingdom of this World*; Farrar, Straus Giroux.
14. De Lisser H. (1929:1982): *The White Witch of Rosehall*: Humanity Press.
15. Roselle Thompson (2018):*The New Folktales & Legends for the 21st Century*: Eagle Publications, London.
16. Mary Shelley (1818:2003) *Frankenstein*: Penguin Classics, UK.
17. **Mama Diablese** – La Diablese (*pronounced La-ja-bless*), is a "Devil woman", who roams around at night. She takes the form of a beautiful woman with eyes like burning coals and a face which resembles a corpse. She hides it under a beautiful wide-brimmed hat and a veil over her face. She might appear beautiful but there is always something that betrays her – the clover hood and her unmistakable laugh. She turns up at village dances, where she is immediately disliked by the women present, but she charms the men and then asks one of them to take her home. He follows her, whilst under her spell, into the woods and then suddenly she disappears. Unable to find his way home, the man stumbles around in the dark wood, until he either falls into a ravine or river to his death or gets attacked by wild hogs.
18. **Oedipus** - Greek Mythology - Oedipus was the son of Laius and Jocasta, king, and queen of Thebes, who, raised by the king of Corinth, later returns to Thebes, and unwittingly kills his father and marries his mother.

19. **Obeah woman** – A woman who practices sorcery, witchcraft, or folk medicine in the Caribbean. Obeah is one of the oldest of all Afro-Creole religions in the Caribbean. Its name is derived from the Ashanti words *Obay-ifo* or *Obeye,* meaning wizard or witch.
20. **Machiavellian** – a person who is a schemer, characterized by subtle or unscrupulous cunning, deception, expediency, and dishonesty.
21. Charlotte Bronte (1847): *Jane Eyre*; Smith, Elder & Co. of London, England, under the pen name "Currer Bell."
22. **Duppy** – This is a word used in various Caribbean islands, originally from Africa, which means a ghost or spirit. They are regarded as malevolent spirits which come out and haunt people at night.
23. Hall S. (2000): *Cultural Representation & Signifying Practices*: Sage Publications, London.
24. Thomas J. J. (1869:1969): *Theory and Practice of Creole Grammar,* New Beacon Books, London & Trinidad.
25. **French Creole Expression** – Sese Mwen, ca c'est comess, oui! *(My dear, this is a real messy confusion, entanglement, and muddle, yes!)*
26. Allsop R. (1996,2003;2010): *Dictionary of Caribbean English Usage*; New York, OUP.
27. Kwéyòl Dictionary (2001);compiled by Paul Crosbie, David Frank, Emanuel Leon, Peter Samuel; Ed. David Frank; Ministry of Education, Government of St. Lucia. **ALSO,** *A Dictionary OF Jamaican English* (2002): F.G. Cassidy (Ed) R.B. LePage (Ed). University of the West Indies. **ALSO,** Stephanie Ovide (1996*) Creole-English/English-Creole (Caribbean)*: Concise Dictionary, Hippocrene Books.
28. www.loopnewscaribbean.com
29. Glissant E. (1997): *The Poetics of Relation*: University of Michigan. USA.
30. Benitez-Rojo A. (1992):*The Repeating Island: The Caribbean and the Postmodern Perspective,* Duke University Press.

THE PHANTOM OF THE GREAT HOUSE

CHARACTERS

George McDonald, Owner of the Great House

Mary McDonald, George's wife

Stella Gregory, an English woman of Grenadian descent

Alex, *Stella's Fiancé*

Andrew, *Alex's business colleague*

James, *Alex's business colleague*

Julie, *Stella's best friend*

Airport Taxi Drivers

Cinnamon Hotel Receptionist

Little Chris, *local taxi driver*

Mama Lola, *Obeah Woman*

Ruth Long, *past Senior maid at the Great House*

Daisy Patrick, *past Senior maid at the Great House*

A Work-Hand, *Chaperone to McDonald*

A Government Minister

A Priest

A Doctor

Jane, Claudette, Ivy & Angel, *George McDonald's mistresses*

Anancy
Cricket   **The Chorus**
Papa Bois
Frog
Firefly

Locations: London, Grenada.

1.1   THE PHANTOM OF THE GREAT HOUSE

ACT 1 SCENE 1 – LONG TIME WE DOH FETE LIKE THIS!

IN THE CARIBBEAN – *outdoors, in the backyard of a Great House, in the moonlight. A group of Caribbean icons, gather around a fire, roasting corn, making Asham, (powdery dried corn mixed with sugar), peeling provisions, (yam, sweet potato, breadfruit, dasheen) for a cook-up, which they are having, whilst liming. The group consists of the usual folktale night-time friends, those who usually witness the folks' storytelling;* **(firefly, cricket, frog, Papa Bois as bolee tree,** *and* **Anancy)** *as they narrate the past events surrounding the Great House.*
A cooking pot is on an open-fire, with ground-provisions cooking. Nearby, there is a mortar with dry corn and a long pestle. The friends gather around in a semi-circle. Soft steel-pan music playing in the background. Using the storytelling tradition, they take turns to narrate the story and function as **a Chorus** *in the play's* **Crick! Crack!** *storytelling fashion, in the Caribbean.*

CRICKET   Leh me fly and rest right here on this big leaf and hear what all-you got to say about this big old Great House over there. *(He motions to the old building nearby).* In fact, of all the places we could go, why we choose to come here at the back of this old, haunted house to do our cook-up? The thing is, they say a phantom lurks in this *Great House,* right there.

PAPA BOIS   *(fanning the fire)* Ah hear it's so sinister, we can expect it to keep repeatin' the past misery to any man or woman who think they want to come and live in it. That's why you doh see nobody comin' here. In fact, you see that place there, ah sure it's jus' waiting for the next victims, to turn their lives upside down; jus' like the ones in the past.
(The others draw close and start turning the roasted corn on the open fire).

1.1 THE PHANTOM OF THE GREAT HOUSE

FROG Man, that *Great House* is really cursed. At night-time, believe me, ah sure ah could even hear cries, voices that sound so sad like hearts breakin' for sure. Some even say they seen ghosts in the windows. As for seeing ghosts, ah doh know, eh - you know how stories does fly around, anyhow with gossip.

ANANCY *(pounding corn in a mortar with a pestle)* Well, as all-you know, I am *Keeper* of these tales and I know them well. For instance, I know talk of unexplained disappearances, from that same house, murder, mischief, and trickery, and believe me, death still pervades the atmosphere inside there.

CRICKET *(blowing the smoke)* This cook-up smellin' good, ah just put in some onions. *(stirs the cook-up pot)* Now, as for me, hidin' during the daytime in dark corners, ah could hear rumours of the past comess that went on inside that house. The horrors almost seem like they penetrated the very walls and even the broken windows flapping in their broken frames. *(tastes the sauce with a big spoon, he winces)* Umm!

ANANCY So, how the cook-up tastin', man?

CRICKET Well, ah think it need a tiny bit more salt. *(Puts in some salt and points to the Great House)* You see that Great House over there, sometimes, when you look at it, it's like everythin' about it is scary. Like it angry, and it doh look welcomin', eh. *(pointing to Firefly).* Firefly, ah bet you doh even fly too close to that House. After all, what you would need to go in there for?

FIREFLY *(fanning the wooden fire and coughing from the smoke)* You see me, *(coughs again)*, Ah stayin' well away from that place. Those echoes and nightly groans you seem to hear from door

1.1   THE PHANTOM OF THE GREAT HOUSE

                    hinges, and ah hear there is damp, musky smells of dead bodies and rottin' floorboards inside there; that will scare anybody. *(pauses).* Ah puttin' in the dumplin' now, eh?

PAPA BOIS *(motioning with his hand)* Go ahead, man. Put in a little chive, thyme, and some salt butter in there too, eh.

FIREFLY And, as for the empty rooms and corridors, they seem to mock the past residents. They say all their possession is still inside there, just as they left them. Fancy that? Once they had all the power, to own the land, as far as your eyes could see from here. Now what they have? S-T-U-P-E-S!

CRICKET Yes, these Planter-owners did take everythin' for themselves. They make people here work like donkey to maintain their estate, and keep them in subjugation and fear. Then, with all their greatness and fancy lifestyle, they create enough mêlée here, before they all fall from grace.

PAPA BOIS I agree with you, then they take their hoity-toity self and leave the island, puttin' Overseers to manage the place. Easily, they exit, becomin' absentee landlords.

FIREFLY Exactly! *(laughing)* But you mean they run away! Because guess what, the joke is on them!

PAPA BOIS Yeh, man, the joke is on them, because even their Overseein' Supervisors run away too! *(laughs)* It's because of all the bad luck and catastrophe that damn *ghost house* cause!

FIREFLY Is a ghost house, oui!

PAPA BOIS Ah tellin' all-you, that's what I call it, a *ghost house*. In any case, why did they call it *Great House,* What's *'great'* about it? Because right now, instead of people livin' there, it's a *Phantom* that take over. *(hands some roasted corn to Frog)*

1.1 THE PHANTOM OF THE GREAT HOUSE

FROG *(takes the corn-cob and bites it)* T'anks. Yes, it's true, when I come out to *lime* around this pond here in the night, lyin' there takin' in the moonlight, I listen to the *sweet-sweet talk* of lover-boys, mamaguyin' girls in the bushes, with all kinda stories.

PAPA BOIS *(laughing)* Yeah man! ah like to hear sweet-talk, too! *(The group laughs with bravado)*

FROG But, sometimes, is lie they lyin', you know. You hear fellas re-tellin' stories, when they feelin' really nice, and want to show off to the woman, they desperate to catch; *(laughs)* You hear them addin' their own drama to the stories, until the girl gets captivated. Hear them noh, *"sweet cheeks, doodoo chile, chookaloonks!"* *(laughs)* and bam! Before you know it, the man done have his way with her.

CRICKET Well, every rope gat two ends, that's what old folks say. *(laughs and shakes his head)* Brer Anancy, how's that *Asham* comin' along, you takin' too long to pound that corn. I hungry man, how come, it's not ready yet? *(walks over to where Anancy is pounding)* And another thing, some even say late at night, they see a Mama La Diablese, around that Great house. You know, the Devil woman with one human leg and one cow foot, who roams around at night. You believe in that, Firefly?

FIREFLY *(stirring the pot)* Hold on, noh! Food ready now. Take the other bottle of rum from the bag over there and bring your plate because ah sharin'. Papa Bois, you're the oldest, so come up first. *(He shares food into each bowl then pauses)* Now, going back to answer your question; well, let's jus' say, ah believe what the old folks say.

1.1   THE PHANTOM OF THE GREAT HOUSE

And trust me, ah hear this story a million times before!

CRICKET *(blowing into his bowl and eating)* Man, ah hear fellas say this *Mama La Diablese* takes the form of a beautiful woman, sexy looking, she have one cow foot! With she big breasts showing, wearin' a hat, beautiful clothes, and eyes like burnin' coals, but one thing eh, she face look like a corpse! *(laughs loudly)* Ha, ha, hai!! But a cow foot? Me, ah doh know about that one for sure, because hear noh? *(pauses and whispers)* Ah doh get to see what's below she dress yet!
(the group roars with laughter)

PAPA BOIS All-you think is joke, he jokin'! I hear with me own ears, the folks say every night, a *Mama La Diablese* does roam up and down the place, lamentin' the loss of her baby in childbirth, caused by a man she did love once.

FROG *(nodding)* Yeah, ah hear that too. They say she died of a broken heart, and now she clanking a chain of bondage, draggin' it behind her every night, and terrorisin' any man she meet. She lures them into the woods and then kill them, for revenge. In fact, they say it's the Madam of this *Great House*, who turn into a *Mama La Diablese*! But ah go tell all-you her story another time eh, leh me eat me food now, ah hungry.

PAPA BOIS *(eating food from his bowl)* It's true, what all-you sayin', because as *Father of the forest,* I even had to save an innocent young man one night, from her grasp. That night, ah could see her comin', then as soon as she see the bwoy, she hide in the bushes, coverin' her cow foot. She start fixin' herself by pushin' up her big-breast chest to mamaguy the poor boy. Himself he walkin' along, lookin' love-struck, like he glidin' on air. You

1.1 THE PHANTOM OF THE GREAT HOUSE

know, maybe he just left his sweetheart, but he wasn't lookin' where he's goin'. I watch her as she try to make her play. So, ah quickly shapeshift into a wild boar, just to cut across the path to distract him and prevent her from destroyin' that poor bwoy. It was his lucky night, for sure. Man, she jus' disappear, poof! into thin air!

ANANCY U-hmm! *(clears his throat and stands)* Well, as the *Keeper* of these folktales, I have news for all-you. The winds of change are blowin' this way. *(shading his eyes and looking around)* They blowin' in someone from a far distant land, to come right here, in this Great House, again! *(pauses)* And by the way, leh me say, the corn-dumplin' was just right, that food taste good man, and congratulations for whoever takin' credit for it tonight.

FROG *(half whispering)* Brer Anancy, ah doh mean to question you, but you *sure* somebody's comin' *here,* in this haunted place, *again*?

ANANCY Yeh man, I tell you that person is comin', all the way from England. And is a woman too! Ah telling all-you she's comin' right here! Yep, comin' to claim that ghostly, ageless, documenter of histories, standin' right over there. *(Pointing to the Great House).* That concrete guard on duty for life, that relic of a lot of past hurt and pain. *(Looking at the others and nodding his head)* Yeh, she's comin' *right here*, and real soon too!

FIREFLY A woman! Bon Dieu, Papa Gawd oh, help the poor thing!

FROG *(rising, he puts his bowl down)* Well, ah sorry to say, but she's comin' as a lamb to the slaughter, that's for sure!

1.1 THE PHANTOM OF THE GREAT HOUSE

PAPA BOIS *(shakes his head in disbelief and puts his bowl down)* Oh well, another one bite the dust, eh!

ANANCY *(rubbing his stomach as he stands)* Well, Firefly, as the main cook, that food was one of the best, I did only pound corn to make the *Asham,* not too much of a challengin' job. So, comrades, compliments on the best cook-up evenings in a long time, we must do it again soon, eh.

FROG Yes we must, that's one of the good things about fellas limin,' it's like a family coming together.

ANANCY *(surveying the surroundings)* Now, goin' back to the news of the comin' visitor, I see what all-you mean, because this place just seems to ruin anyone who think they're brazen enough to venture into this relic of stench, death, destruction, and the broken lives it done mash up already. Well, is come she comin', and in true story-tellin' fashion, we going to open the curtain and let all-you see how the Phantom of this Great House rises, and strikes again. So leh me start by saying, **CRICK!**

AUDIENCE & CHORUS ***CRACK!***

[Curtains

1.2   THE PANTOM OF THE GREAT HOUSE

ACT 1 SCENE 2 – A FORTUNE FROM FAR AWAY!

In a local bar in London. Stella talks to her best friend Julie about her sudden change of fortunes. The women are served drinks at a table. Lights are dim, apart from spotlights on the women. Soft music is being played in the background.

STELLA *(excited the friends embrace)* Jules, Thanks for coming! Still can't believe my luck, I feel like I'm going crazy. Please pinch me and tell me I'm not dreaming!

JULIE *(excited and impatient)* So what's happening, tell me all the details. All I could make out from your screams and excitement over the phone is, you're now the owner of an estate, lots of money, and a Mansion in the Caribbean!

STELLA Yes, it's like winning the lottery! Got up one morning, a pretty ordinary day, preparing for work, nothing on my mind, when there was a knock on my front door, together with my doorbell ringing - you know, an impatient ring. I opened the door and there stood the postman with a registered letter that I had to sign for.

JULIE *(rubbing her hands excitedly)* Go on!

STELLA I still can't believe it - It was a letter from a Lawyer, the Executor of a Will. He said in the letter they'd been looking for me for years, and as the only surviving next of kin, of a fortune that had been left in a Will for me, I had to go to their UK office with ID documents to identify myself.

JULIE Is this for real? I trust you! You checked it out, right?

STELLA Well, my dear, I have legal documents, which I checked out with my own legal people and yep, it's legit alright!

JULIE *(giggling)* So, what happens now? What does Alex have to say about all this? And how you're

1.2   THE PHANTOM OF THE GREAT HOUSE

	going to manage your fortune in the Caribbean, from here in England?
STELLA	*(grimaces)* Well, that's the little snag I want to pick your brains about. Alex is sceptical. He doesn't trust what he calls 'foreign property and strangers offering me a fortune.' He says it seems too good to be true! In fact, he doesn't seem to want to me accept it at all!
JULIE	So, what you saying? He doesn't want you to get involved!
STELLA	Jules, I can't figure him out, right now. Since I've told him, he's kind ah acting strange, you know.
JULIE	*(frowns)* Is it jealousy? What d'you mean, "acting strange"?
STELLA	Well, let's just say, he says he has a hunch there's something not right about this sudden change of fortune, that it feels uneasy, says he feels heart palpitations and fearful! In any case, he doesn't think we need it, since his business is really doing well.
JULIE	*(pokes Stella)* Lucky you!
STELLA	Well, we have money saved for our wedding; everything is taken care of. We've worked our socks off and our future is quite secure, really. But his overall objection is his *hunch* of something ominous about the whole thing.
JULIE	Wow! And you Stella, what d'you think? Are you saying you don't need any more money?
STELLA	No, no, I'm not saying that, but I don't know! I feel there's something that I need to sort out, you know, once and for all. Like, questions to be asked and answers are needed. In fact, I believe I need to lay a ghost of this past to rest.
JULIE	*(hesitates)* O.K.
STELLA	*(frowns)* I need closure on this whole idea of *family* and this *family legacy* business. You know,

1.2 THE PHANTOM OF THE GREAT HOUSE

	you don't just turn your back on a fortune just like that, because of someone's uneasy hunch! I need to show responsibility, by going and checking out the history behind this fortunate reality!
JULIE	*(raising up her hand)* OK, so when are you going?
STELLA	*(smiling coyly)* I didn't say anything about *going* yet!
JULIE	C'm on Alex, I know you long enough to know you plan to go. *(laughing)* So what's been arranged so far? And when you leaving?
STELLA	*(excitedly)* Well, I got a flight booked for next weekend from Heathrow to Grenada. Listen Jules, Alex hasn't said it, but I sense this trip will either rock our relationship real hard or maybe it might even break it.
JULIE	Hmm! It's that bad, huh?
STELLA	Kinda, but trying to be positive, I'm banking on the fact that he'll come round to the whole idea, once I go and come back and he finds that everything's worked out just right!
JULIE	You know what I always say; you and Alex are two strong-headed, defiant, never-giving-up, two-of-a-kind type of couple. He won't budge, and you won't budge either; I know you guys well.
STELLA	*(sighing)* Yes, yes, you got that right!
JULIE	But listen, I'm your best friend – and all I'll say is, be extra careful, at all times, especially while you're out there. Things aren't always what they seem.
STELLA	Thanks Jules, I knew you'd understand. 'll only be gone for 4 weeks.
JULIE	*(smiling reassuringly, she touches her shoulder)* OK go, if you really must! But you know I'm always here for you, whenever you need.

1.2 THE PHANTOM OF THE GREAT HOUSE

STELLA *(touching her heart)* You're the best! *(Sighs)* And what about you?
JULIE *(shrugs)* Nothing much has changed!
STELLA C'm on, let's have another drink and tell me everything about your own news. Alex won't be home for a while yet – he's meeting Andrew and James after work.

[Curtains

ACT 1 SCENE 3 – THE PHANTOM IS STIRRING!

London: Alex, Andrew, and James are in a local bar, going over some papers. The men are co-workers, engaged in a discussion. They are sitting around a table with drinks, in a bar, perusing documents. Quiet classical musical plays in the background.

JAMES	OK, just to re-cap, am I right in saying that we all agree with this contract, and the cost of the stock?
ALEX & ANDREW	Check!
JAMES	We also agreed on the length of time, delivery dates.
ALEX & ANDREW	Check!
JAMES	We've considered the impact of possible force majeure, or disruptions to the contract delivery time, and we're all happy with, bottom line – the contract price.
ALEX & ANDREW	Yep!
JAMES	*(closes his notepad, slaps his pen down on the table)* So, to conclude, you're saying we're going ahead with this contract, right?
ANDREW	Yes, all sounds good to me! OK, gentlemen, since we have a deal on the table, that calls for a drink!
JAMES	Listen guys, none for me. I'd love to stop and have another drink but tonight is daddy-duty night. I promised Susie I'll be home in time to put Jack to bed – you know, *(winks at his friends)* My turn to read the bedtime story. *(Taking his coat to leave)* But I'll catch you guys at the weekend!

[Exit James

1.3 THE PHANTOM OF THE GREAT HOUSE

ANDREW *(catches the barman's gaze and motions him)* Same again, Alex?

ALEX Something stronger, like double scotch, and neat!

ANDREW Wow! that's not like you! Double Scotch! If I didn't know you, I'd say you were celebrating something or, priming up yourself for something special later, eh! *(teasing)* Nudge, nudge, wink, wink, you know!

ALEX To be honest, there is something on my mind, but I can't really say that I'm celebrating it. Nah, not at all. In fact, that kind a thing scares the life out of me. Look, see it's already sending me to drink alcohol like this.

ANDREW *(jokingly)* Wow! Wow! You're not serious?

ALEX Ah! Believe me, you won't understand.

ANDREW *(looking at his friend seriously)* You *are* serious! So what's it then, c'm on, spill out the beans! *(pauses pointing to Alex laughing),* Hold on! Don't tell me yet, let me guess, Stella is pregnant. Yes?

ALEX No, *that* would be a simple one to come to terms with and certainly celebrate but...*(shakes his head).*

ANDREW OK, so try me! We've been buddies since school days, and I think I can sense when something's not right. Look, I noticed you weren't as sharp this evening in our meeting. C'm on, something's on your mind, let's hear it. *(pauses)* That is, if you feel like sharing it.

ALEX Warning, it will sound crazy, but the truth is, I don't know how to respond to something that's happened to Stella.

ANDREW *(Thoughtfully shaking his head)* OK, go on!

ALEX Stella's come into a fortune from a family – and apparently, she's the only surviving next of kin, and

	yeah, it's a big deal. It's as if she's suddenly won the lottery! A mansion, a huge Estate and lots of money.
ANDREW	Fantastic news! *(Looking puzzled)* And you're ***not*** celebrating this good fortune?
ALEX	It's not as simple as that, and besides, it's not even in this country; but yes, it's all hers! I know I should be happy but somehow, I just can't help feeling uneasy about the whole thing. To be honest, my gut reaction is fear. I have nightmares about this and then I wake up in a cold sweat. Haven't told Stella any of this. *(shaking his head)* I just don't know, but I think that she should refuse it!
ANDREW	*(Surprised)* Refuse a fortune! C'm on Alex, what's so wrong about taking a fortune that's given, freely?
ALEX	See, I told you, I knew you wouldn't understand. The thing is, I just can't rationalise my feelings. But something tells me all this would end upside down! She's bent on going to the Caribbean to claim her *prize*, so to speak. She knows nothing about the Caribbean, it's not like she's just going to Cornwall or Isle of Wight. And besides, we already have enough of everything; we really don't need anything else to complicate our lives.
ANDREW	Wait, something's not making sense to me. You want her to turn down a fortune because it's not located close by, or you want Stella to refuse it because it doesn't *feel* right!
ALEX	Something like that!
ANDREW	OK, but it ***is*** legit, right?
ALEX	Yes, it's legal. We had it checked out by a lawyer, but I don't understand how, or why, I'm feeling so uncomfortable, it's just a hunch, and I can't quite put my finger on it.

1.3   THE PHANTOM OF THE GREAT HOUSE

ANDREW Hmm! Sounds like you two need to talk, and I Mean *really* talk seriously about this some more.

ALEX Look, I've tried but we're arguing a lot. In fact, I feel I might be pushing her away from me. Things haven't been going right lately. The thing is, since this damn legacy landed in our letterbox, so to speak, it's done nothing but divided our feelings – I don't know, but to me, something just doesn't feel right.

ANDREW *(nodding)* I hear you.

ALEX *(lowers voice)* Between you and me, the last time I had similar feelings, it took place sometime before I got news of my twin brother's mysterious death, on a vacation in Cuba. This same weird feeling had occurred weeks before the news arrived!

ANDREW *(looking worried, but consolatory)* OK, tell you what, why don't we go and have a meal, somewhere quieter, and maybe we could try to unravel this little puzzle together. How about it?

ALEX Yes, by all means, let's go. I'll do anything to shake off this ominous feeling about this damned fortune. It just doesn't feel right, you know.

ANDREW OK, don't worry, let's go, we'll talk it through together.

[Curtains

ACT 2 SCENE 1 – CHASING THE PHANTOM

At Point Salines Airport. Stella arrives in Grenada.
On a Taxi concourse, outside the airport building, Taxi Drivers are touting for passengers. There is a flurry of activities among newly-arrived passengers.

DRIVER 1 *(waving his hand)* Taxi! Madam, Welcome to our beautiful Caribbean island, I can take you anywhe' you want to go!

STELLA *(approaches confidently)* Thank You! I'm going to the Great House on St. John's Hill.

DRIVER 1 *(backing away in surprise)* Eh-Eh! Me? No Madam! Not that place, Ah not goin' there!
[Exits

STELLA *(approaches 2nd driver)* Hi, are you going anywhere near St. John's Hill?

DRIVER 2 St. John Hill, yes.

STELLA Good. I want to go to the Great House.

DRIVER 2 *(he makes the sign of the cross on himself)* The Great House! That Place, madam? You sure? *(Frightened, he backs away from Stella),* No, no, not me, madam
[Exits

STELLA *(walks towards another driver)* Well, then, how about you? I'm going to the Great House.

DRIVER 3 The Great House? S-t-u-p-e-s! *(walks away shouting)* So you think is stupid, ah stupid, eh?
[Exits

STELLA *(shows a $50 note to 4th driver)* Driver, look, I'll give you this extra $50, on top of your fare, if you'll take me to my address.

DRIVER 4 Wait, you mean you givin' me $50, plus the fare ah goin' to charge you when we get there, right?

STELLA Yes, here is the $50 as tip now. I'll give you the fare when we arrive.

2.1 THE PHANTOM OF THE GREAT HOUSE

DRIVER 4 *(excitedly pockets the money)* Thanks! Here, leh me take your bags. I'll put them in the trunk. *(Rapidly opens passenger door)* Here, madam, please sit down inside. *(Happily, jumps in front the steering wheel and starts the engine).* Now, whe' you want to go?

STELLA Thank you, *(Handing him the address on a piece of paper)* Please, take me to this address, d'you know it?

DRIVER 4 *(he turns off the car engine abruptly)* Madam! But that's de old Great House! You sure dis is whe' you goin'? You know you cyan go inside there right! *(He hands her back the piece of paper with address)*

STELLA *(laughing casually)* What d'you mean, I can't go in there? But that's where I've come to stay.

DRIVER 4 What! You're sayin' you come to *stay* there? Pure madness!

STELLA I beg your pardon?

DRIVER 4 Ah mean, let's jus' say that place is a no-go area. Madam, d'you know anybody on dis island? That place is abandoned - must be at least 10 years now!

STELLA I see, so you're saying I can't sleep in there tonight, because it's not clean.

DRIVER 4 No, no no, ah sayin' you cyan sleep in there, period. In fact, you cyan sleep tonight or any other night! Madam, how come you want to go there?

STELLA Wow! I see. It's that bad huh! Ok, it might need a little cleanin' and sprucin' up; I can understand that.

[Curtains

DRIVER 4 Sprucin'? Madam, whe' you come from? It needs more than sprucin' up! It need Madam Lola, she's like ah exorcist, you know, the local

2.1 THE PHANTOM OF THE GREAT HOUSE

DRIVER 4: obeah woman! *(Laughing nervously)* Look, ah go take you to the nearest house-hotel to that place, but ah not going to that Great House.

STELLA: *(ponders thoughtfully)* OK, then take me to a hotel nearby, by all means, but please drive the same route as the Great House, I'd like to have a quick glance, as we go past.

DRIVER 4: Sorry madam, It's not on my route. I can take you to Cinnamon Spice hotel, a real nice little place; it's 20-minute drive from whe' you want to go.

STELLA: O.K. If it's only 20 minutes away from the Great House, then yes, take me to the Cinnamon Spice.

DRIVER 4: *(cagily eyes Stella from his rear-view mirror)* Look, takin' you to Cinnamon Spice Hotel will cost you another $50 and it's not that ah doh trust you, but please give me the fare now, as well?

STELLA: *(agitated, sighs loudly)* OK, if you people *really* must have it all *your* way, but can you at least tell me, before you drive off, what is it about the Great House, that seem to spook you and all the other drivers so much?

DRIVER 4: You really mean you doh know? *(shakes head)* Madam, that place is doomed a long time ago!

STELLA: *(gives the fare)* I hear you, but one last favour. Do you know where I can find someone called Ruth Long or Daisy Patrick? I believe these two women used to work in the *Great House* for a long time.

DRIVER 4: No, Madam! Ah doh know anyone like that. *(hurriedly)* And ah really have to go, right now.

[Curtains

2.2 THE PHANTOM OF THE GREAT HOUSE

ACT 2 SCENE 2 – YOUNG, WITH GUTS LIKE COBO

A morning at the Cinnamon Spice Hotel: Stella wakes up and looks out of her bedroom window. She sees a strange-looking, one-eyed, old man, with a hat, at the back looking up, staring at her window. As soon as she opens the window, he immediately disappears.

RECEPTIONIST Madam, Welcome to the Cinnamon, how was your 1st night and your breakfast?

STELLA Thanks for asking, I slept like a log, was very tired after that long-haul flight. Can you call me a taxi please. I'd like to go to St. John's Hill.

RECEPTIONIST No problem, M'am, one will be here in 5 minutes.

STELLA Great! I'll wait outside, such a lovely sunny day, we don't have many of those in London except summer. I'm going to make the most of it, while I'm here.

RECEPTIONIST *(laughing)* Well, sunshine is something we sure have plenty of all the time but sometimes too much of one thing is not good too!

STELLA *(at the hotel entrance)* Are you the Cab for St. John's Hill?

DRIVER Yes, Madam.

STELLA Well, it's for me!

DRIVER *(opens the car door)* Please, take a seat.

STELLA *(enters & sits at the rear)* Thank you.

DRIVER *(pops his head in the Hotel entrance, waves to the Receptionist)*
Where to, in St. John Hill please?

STELLA Well, I don't know the area, but do you know the Great House, I am going near there.

DRIVER Near there, sure! But I can only go as far as the bridge and then you will have to walk about 10 minutes, up the hill. You OK with that?

STELLA But, why not in front of the Great House?

2.2   THE PHANTOM OF THE GREAT HOUSE

DRIVER   Madam, the road is blocked, up there is like an over-grown jungle surrounding that place and nobody ever goes there. There is no usable driving path for almost a decade now!

STELLA   I see, would I be able to walk up to the Great House?

DRIVER   Madam, I really can't tell you that. Why don't you get someone to go with you? You seem to be taking quite a risk, after all the past horror in the place. In fact, you won't get anyone even coming as far as I have.

STELLA   Really? Why not?

DRIVER   *(smiling)* Today must be your lucky day, because after las' night, I'm in a pretty good mood.

STELLA   That's good to know!

DRIVER   And I have to say, with all the rumours and stories about ghosts haunting there, I was only a child when all that carnage took place there, so it's neither here nor there to me. Superstition, you know!

STELLA   A past carnage, did you say?

DRIVER   *(jovially boasting)* Yes m'am, rumour has it that if you go there you might not make it back, so no one goes there. In fact, no one wants to take the chance - they say it's haunted. At least, that's what I heard, but I aint one to believe in the old tales by the folks.

STELLA   Nor me, folktales don't frighten me!

DRIVER   Folktales, whatever they say about them, is just 'Nancy stories to me. Forget about all that superstitious nonsense.

STELLA   That's right!

DRIVER   In fact, the younger generation, like me, just want to make life. You know, after finishing school, travelling abroad is the next best thing. So, I

2.2 THE PHANTOM OF THE GREAT HOUSE

	intend to make a better life too. You know, like you!
STELLA	Travelling *is* good, yes, but I didn't travel abroad, I live abroad.
DRIVER	Well, look at you - young, good looking, you came here all by yourself – so you're free to do whatever you want, isn't it! As for me, for sure, someday soon, I'm going to leave this place and go to America.
STELLA	*(shaking her head in agreement)* Yes, and why not? But I'm not from America, I'm from London. Now, tell me, is this your own Taxi?
DRIVER	Yes, ma'm! This is my very own car. You see, I'm my own boss. I work when I want to or *lime* with them fellas, *(laughing)* and also play with the girls – when I want to!
STELLA	*(pondering)* So, as your own boss, you will be open to a daily hire, to take me around whilst I'm here on the island, yes?
DRIVER	*(grinning)* Madam, If the price is right, I'm at your service! Island tours, party tours, shopping tours. Anywhere-you-want-tours! *(cheekily, flashing his teeth in a wide smile)* Even anything-you-want-tours!
STELLA	OK, sound's good. But on one condition - that I would need you as my driver, as well as a Chaperone. I mean, be there when I want you; you know, a constant companion to show me the ropes.
DRIVER	Ropes, which ropes?
STELLA	*(laughing)* There's no rope, I don't mean that literally. It's a British saying, means you have to familiarise me with everything. I need to know about everything on this island, especially the Great House. So, for $150 a day, is it a deal?

2.2 THE PHANTOM OF THE GREAT HOUSE

DRIVER *(animated)* Madam, I'd say for $200 a day, you got yourself a *real good* deal with *Little Chris* at your service! *(motions for a handshake)*

STELLA *(shakes hands and sighs)* OK, Little Chris, it's a deal. My name is Stella, and we start from right now. Park the car and come with me up the hill. We're going to the Great House.

LITTLE CHRIS *(quizzically)* Tell me something Miss Stella, you mean you really don't know anybody on this island?

STELLA *(looks away, hand shading her eyes from the sun)* Nope, I'm afraid so. Not a single soul!
[**Aside**] At least none that I know of!

LITTLE CHRIS *(upbeat)* Well Miss Stella, never fear, 'cause Little Chris is right here!

STELLA Please drop the *Miss,* just call me Stella.

LITTLE CHRIS *(jokingly salutes)* OK Stella, right now, your Little Chris is at your service!

*[**Curtains**]*

ACT 2 SCENE 3 - THE PHANTOM RIDES AGAIN!

In the grounds of the Great House. Overgrown, twisted bushes choke any semblance of path or yard. A sad desolate atmosphere, where eerie silence prevails. The House, a dilapidated greyish structure looms over a jungle that surrounds it. Silhouette of tall bushes in a background of blue lighting is shown.

LITTLE CHRIS   Stella, you sure you still want to keep going. You're not dressed for this little forest hike. So, you'll have to step where I step, as I break the bushes in front me, to make a path.

STELLA   *(determined)* Yep, I'm good to go, we'll keep going, thanks.

LITTLE CHRIS   OKay, it's your call, I'm at your service, though I can't see what good this trek is, insisting on going to a bruk-up, falling down, old shell of a house, in this blasted hot sun.

STELLA   *(pointing to the right)* Oh Look! There's an old man over there? How did he get here and what's he doing there?

LITTLE CHRIS   *(turns around sharply)* What man? *(straining to see)* I can't see anyone.

STELLA   Yes, an old man, with one eye, he was wearing a hat. He was standing over there, looking at us. In fact, it's the same man I saw this morning, outside my bedroom window, at the hotel.

LITTLE CHRIS   You sure, you did see someone just now?

STELLA   Of course, I definitely saw him over there. *(she points)*

LITTLE CHRIS   OK, so, where's he gone? How come I don't see anyone now?

STELLA   I don't know why!

LITTLE CHRIS   And why would he be outside your hotel bedroom window? What for?

2.3 THE PHANTOM OF THE GREAT HOUSE

STELLA I don't know, but he looks very distinctive. Because he's very old and wrinkled, with one eye patch, with strange looks, and had a hat on.

LITTLE CHRIS *(teasing)* Hey, little English lady, don't let the sun get to you, or catch sunstroke. You know what they say about mad dogs and Englishmen.

STELLA *(laughing)* Nope, I don't know what they say, but we'll keep going - the house is just ahead of us now.

LITTLE CHRIS Well for your information, the Englishmen when they come to our hot countries, behave as if they're mad. They go outside in the mid-day sun when it's at its hottest, when every sensible person in the land, stays in the shade and waits for the strongest sun to pass, before going out again. But for me, I would say we could go back anytime you want, eh.

STELLA Nope, no turning back now, just keep going!

LITTLE CHRIS Oh Gawd! *(pointing)* I see trouble over there!

STELLA What trouble?

LITTLE CHRIS *(lowers his voice)* Now Stella, I want you to move *very slowly* and follow every move I make because we just have to. *(Points & whispers)* There's a real big serpent coiled up on a branch over there.

STELLA *(fearful, whispers back)* Wh-Wh-Where?

LITTLE CHRIS It's over there. But as long as we just pass *real* slow, it shouldn't bother us. Hold on to my waist, follow me, step by step. Move s-l-o-w-l-y.

STELLA *(furiously swats flying insects, having disturbed the tall bushes)* O God, these flies, one just went up my nose! Urrggh! *(Spitting and panicking)* I want to sniff right now! I just have to sneeze!

LITTLE CHRIS *(signalling his hands to his lips for quiet)* OK! Not just yet, eh! *(Pointing to the distance)* We need to get over there, just hold on a minute,

2.3 THE PHANTOM OF THE GREAT HOUSE

otherwise that serpent over there will finish us today.

STELLA *(panic-stricken, holds her nose)* OK, OK, but not for long! Oh! Oh! A-tishooo! A-tishooo!
(Little Chris dives on the ground, to take cover away from the coiled serpent and getting up runs away. Blinded by her sneezes Stella loses her grip on Little Chris and runs around into bushes that are taller than her. They slap her face wildly, as she tries to find him. Struggling with the towering bushes, she thought she felt hands actually touch her, as she falls down a shallow hole)

LITTLE CHRIS *(bending low and whispering)* OK Stella, stop playing games, whe' you is? Because I'm right over here. *(silence - no answer, whispers again)* Stella, it's too dangerous to play around out here, girl. *(no replies for a while)*
(loud yells) Stella! Stella! Stella!
(mumbles to himself) Look at me ass cross, noh! *(breaks a branch and peels the leaves to make a stick)* That damn English woman go and get she-self lost in this blasted forest. *(beating the bush as he walks)* What for, to chase after a big, dirty, stinking, old, bruk-up house she don't know anything about.
(he sees an old man in the distance)
Hey, you, mister! You, over there! Ah looking for a girl - you know, the one you saw early this morning! Whe' she gone?
(he walks towards the man who instantly disappears)
Is this some kind a game-playing? Why is everybody disappearing? If all-you playing a game, I'm not in the mood for playing, you know. *(turning full circle around shouts)* Hey mister! whe' you gone?

2.3 THE PHANTOM OF THE GREAT HOUSE

STELLA *(eerie screams)* Help! Help me! Little Chris! I'm down here! Hello! Can you hear me?

LITTLE CHRIS Stella! Stella! *(mutters to himself)* Oh God, I don't want no trouble today, eh! *(he yells)* Stella! Stella!

STELLA Yes, I'm down here! Help me, Little Chris! I'm down here!

LITTLE CHRIS OK, I hear you now! Down where? *(running in the direction of the sound)*

STELLA Be careful, I fell into a hole. Over here! I'm over here!

LITTLE CHRIS Okay, Okay, thank God! Yes, I hear you now. Oh Stella, thank God! Just a minute, Okay! *(frantically, clearing the area with his bare hand)* I'm coming, hold on! Here, take this stick, hold it, I will pull you out.

STELLA Pull me and I'll push with my legs. *(he pulls)* Pull! Pull, I'm almost there, I'm coming! *(grabs his ankle, kneels, and stands)*

LITTLE CHRIS *(grabs and hugs her to his chest)* Oh Stella, I thought I'd lost you!

STELLA *(frightened she accepts his embrace)* Oh Little Chris, I thought I'd lost you too!

LITTLE CHRIS *(still holding Stella close to him)* I saw him.

STELLA *(loosening his embrace)* Saw who?

LITTLE CHRIS Y'know, the old man you saw earlier this morning, at the hotel.

STELLA You did! See, I told you I'd seen him. Where is he now?

LITTLE CHRIS He just disappeared, exactly as you said; poof, into thin air, like a ghost!

STELLA Well, that was a scary lesson, I thought I felt hands touching me in that thick bush down there. It was so weird. But I still intend to go into that Great House today.

2.3 THE PHANTOM OF THE GREAT HOUSE

LITTLE CHRIS *(staring thoughtfully into her eyes)* Look Stella, I'll continue with you, on one condition, you hold onto me tightly and let me hold you tightly around your waist; that way we won't separate again!

STELLA *(searching his eyes)* Ok, for the next 10 minutes only, because I reckon we'll reach the house in roughly 10 minutes.

LITTLE CHRIS Listen, as you can see, in this strange choking jungle out here, a lot can happen in 10 minutes. *(suddenly sounding upbeat)* But as you say, we going to the Great House, right?

STELLA Yes, we're going right inside it. *(shouts with fist in the air)* So, let's do this!

LITTLE CHRIS *(animated)* Yep, let's do this!

[Curtains

ACT 2 SCENE 4 - WHAT YOU HEAD LEAD YOU TO DO, YOU BACKSIDE GO PAY FOR IT!

Stella and Little Chris enter the unlocked Great House. The contents of the house are still in place since it was last occupied.
There are sounds of a black bird squawking, and bats flying out. Squeaky floor-boards, cobwebs, peeling paint, old furniture covered in dust, in the rotting house is seen. Blue and red lighting, mixed in the background, conveys a sense of mystery.

LITTLE CHRIS	*(pushes the front door)* Wow, it's not locked! It's full of cobwebs. Watch your step, the floor-board's rotten, it have holes. *(steps inside)* Oh Gawd, this place smell like death!
STELLA	*(searching her pocket)* And it's too dark. Let's use the light from my mobile phone.
LITTLE CHRIS	*(treading cautiously)* Everywhere is rotten. So why you insist on coming here?
STELLA	That's what I came to find out!
LITTLE CHRIS	*(puzzled)* Huh! You come all the way from England to come to this pile of rot, to find out why you should come inside this dead house?
STELLA	Well, how shall I say it? Let's just say it's mine, I own it!
LITTLE CHRIS	What! How you mean you own it? This house is *yours*?
STELLA	Like I said, I'm the new owner. Maybe it's a pile of rot, falling apart, a ghost mansion, but it's all mine!
LITTLE CHRIS	Wow! *(startled by escaping bats)* Look out!
STELLA	*(grabs on to his arm)* What's that?
LITTLE CHRIS	It's just bats! You see, even the bats are running away. This place is dangerous. It gives me the creeps. *(points to the next floor)* And look at a big hole in the floor above us.

2.4 THE PHANTOM OF THE GREAT HOUSE

STELLA *(touching the peeling paint and cracked wall)* This place has seen better days, for sure. It has 3 floors but right now, everything is decayed - the walls, broken, water soaked, paint peeling, and it does smell like a dead body's here.

LITTLE CHRIS How come everything's still here? Settees, cabinets, piano, everything packed in boxes, sewing machine, stove, old fridges, even an old clock stopped at 2.09; which day, which year, we don't know, but everything rotting anyway.

STELLA All rotten, for sure.

LITTLE CHRIS Like they left in a hurry and left everything behind. *(He pushes another door)* This one is locked.

STELLA Let's break it open, we need to see what's in there.

LITTLE CHRIS How you know it have a floor in there, suppose we rush in and fall through the broken floors?

STELLA *(peeps through the keyhole, eyes showing fear)* Hush, what's that noise?

LITTLE CHRIS What noise?

STELLA I thought I heard someone crying? *(the light from her mobile phone flickers and dies)*

LITTLE CHRIS Stand aside, let me try to break the door with my body weight.

STELLA *(grabs him tightly)* Look a spider! Get rid of it! Kill it!

LITTLE CHRIS You sacred of a little spider?

STELLA Scared to death of them! *(she hides behind him)* Kill it now!

LITTLE CHRIS *(there's a muffled sound)* Hello! Who's there? It sound like somebody crying, I can hear it, but wait, it seems to be coming from downstairs.

STELLA OK, Hurry and break down the door quickly, and let's get out of here. This place is beginning to give me the creeps too.

2.4 THE PHANTOM OF THE GREAT HOUSE

LITTLE CHRIS You sure you want to go inside this room today, we can always come back another time, with tools and a proper light. Plus, it's getting late, and the light is fading, and we don't have a light to see, to get out of here.

STELLA Yes, but we're here already, just break it open, quickly.

LITTLE CHRIS OK, if you say so. Stand back!
(he charges but the door opens by itself in the middle of his charge; with no flooring in the room, he ends up falling through broken floorboard onto the floor below)

STELLA Oh God, Chris are you OK? *(there's silence)* Chris, you aright?

STELLA *(there's a kerfuffle)* Who's there? Stop it! Who's touching me, get off me! *(screams)* Someone's touching me! Get off me!
(she scrambles to move in the dark to the next floor where Little Chris has fallen but also falls heavily down the broken stairs in the dark and is unconscious).

LITTLE CHRIS *(regains consciousness stumbles around in the darkness)*
Stella, whe' you is? *(no reply, he sits up)* Stella, whe' you gone, girl? Stella! Stella! *(no reply)* Oh God, not again!
(He gropes around in the dark and finds Stella's lying on the ground) Oh, there you are!
(bends over her closely, repeatedly smells her breath to check whether she is breathing. He shakes her, but she's unconscious)

[Curtains

ACT 2 SCENE 5 - PAPA MWEN, CA C'EST COMESS OUI!

*The group **Firefly, Cricket, Frog, Papa Bois,** and **Anancy**
are gathered again to lime. Outside in a yard, the group sit around
in a half-circular space, drinking and chatting. At the same time,
they recount a tale of events at the Great House. Blue stage lighting
with silhouette trees in the background show a night-time
environment with night sounds.*

CRICKET *(Anancy approaches)* Hey Anancy! Wha' happenin' deh man?

ANANCY Comme ci, comme ça, ah takin' it easy.

CRICKET Well as for me, I doh mind our group limin' together but is a long time we doh hear a storytellin' session from the folks. *(shakes his head sadly)* I really miss them folktales man.

ANANCY Me too, but you have to remember, time's changed, the world change too, eh. A lot of people gone away. Books replace storytellin' sessions; television keep people inside, like the groups who used to come out here, and listen to our stories. *(shakes his head sadly)* Yes, a lot has happened over the years. But ah tellin' all-you, it's no good me just keepin' all those stories to myself, who knows, maybe one day ah go burst!

FROG Yeah man, people have to tell them. See how they leave us here, just sittin' in the emptiness out here, by ourselves. Worse still, is every time I try to tell my tadpoles about the old folktales, they laugh at me and say they never hear 'bout no storytellin' by any folks. In fact, they ask me if I makin' all this stuff up! So, you see, even my own tadpoles questionin' our history and laughin' at me too! Imagine that!

FIREFLY Eh-eh! You too? Ah didn' know it happen to you too, I thought it was only me! Man, only the other day, our little fireflies said exactly the same

2.5 THE PHANTOM OF THE GREAT HOUSE

        thing, as your tadpoles! But ah blame it on all this bright, bright electricity light; it sure isn't that cosy and naturally dark anymore.

FROG   And another thing, you can hardly see the moon at night, with all this brightness. In fact, no one goes out for walks these days; they all have TVs, fast cars and every man, woman, and child, doing their own damn thing!

CRICKET   You know, you have a point there!

FIREFLY   I used to like the night-time, man, showin' off my beautiful light, flying here, there; man, jus' flyin' everywhere. You right, even the moon hardly joinin' our night group. It's because no one goin' to see us in all this light. My firelight is no comparison for these changes.

PAPA BOIS   It's so true. That's a sad reflection on how things become. The people abandon us, for sure. Now, some will say t'ings good, and it improvin', but improvin' at what cost? Ah mean, what's the real, real, long-term cost, eh? Old people say, *"The same stone the builder refuse, does become the head corner-stone."*

ANANCY   Well, as for me, I think that by the time they realise it, the cost will be great for sure; no continuity, no folk culture, or writin' our folk history. Instead, we copyin' other people's gibberish; S-T-U-P-E-S! it's all going out of the window fast.

PAPA BOIS   You're right!

ANANCY   And if we not careful, soon people go laugh at our stories and say they didn' even exist! Ah mean, look at everyone? Either walkin' up and down like daytime zombies, chasin' the Yankee dollar or the English pound and some too busy to see what's happenin' right here under their noses, in this land.

2.5   THE PHANTOM OF THE GREAT HOUSE

CRICKET   Doh worry man, that's why we have to show interest in what's happenin' in that *Great House*, as old as it is. You see, people comin' from abroad and in a way, cause a different story to be told. And really, that makes it a *new* kind of tale, not like the old-time tales, but as you say Anancy, the winds of change probably bringin' in a new type of tales for our folks too.

FROG   Then, we must be the ones to witness them, so we can tell them and pass them on, in whatever way we can.

FIREFLY   I agree, the old-time white Planter did his share of damage and gone. What he left is very little and now Anancy say some English woman is comin' here again; who knows, maybe through her, our storytellin' tradition will continue.

ANANCY   Well, in fact, ah have to tell all-you she's already here, and from what I hear, she's even been right up here in these grounds, and inside the Great House too!

CRICKET   She did what!

ANANCY   Yes, yes! I hear she had a man inside the Great House there too! In fact, they say that afterwards, she went hoppin' back to the hotel in shock, with a twisted ankle, and all kind ah strange bruises all over she body.

FROG   Eh-eh? So Duppy done play with her already, then!

ANANCY   Listen, eh, they say after she visit the Great House, by the time she reach back into the Cinnamon hotel, she was looking crazy-crazy, like she seen a real Duppy. And worst of all, ah hear she was angrily tellin' people, she didn' come all the way from England to get assaulted by anyone in the Great House, in the dark!

2.5 THE PHANTOM OF THE GREAT HOUSE

PAPA BOIS Eh-heh! Well, her *ass* go get *salted* for sure, if she comin' here to cause trouble!

FIREFLY *(joking)* Ha, ha, hai! And it go get *pepper* too!

CRICKET Man, she's a poppy show. So, it's like England comin' back here to make more trouble! Well, she better know, Massa Day Done; we only toleratin' up to a point now, eh.

FROG S-T-U-P-E-S! As if we doh have enough problem of our own already.

PAPA BOIS So, when she say she was *assaulted*, what she mean? Who she sayin' really *assaulted* her in the Great House?

FROG *(Laughing)* Does she mean a real person or the phantom?

CRICKET She better doh come playin' the mad English Madam in this old house, all over again. Because everybody know what the first one was like and what she did. Way back then, that old madam, Mrs McDonald, did seduce a poor innocent, local labourer, when she forced him into very compromisin' situations, abuse him, then when things got too hot to handle, they kill him!

PAPA BOIS Man, that was real comess in this place! Yes, that business was gossip sensation on the grapevine everywhere. Imagine, the mistress of the house havin' an affair behind her husband back, right on his estate, for all to see. Man, she had no shame!

ANANCY Well, you know you can find Anancy, everywhere. At that time, I even heard the House staff pleadin' with the labourer, to disobey the white woman, scared that her husband would cut the bwoy neck. I hear her with me own ears, scolding him one day. Hear them for yourselves.

FLASHBACK: *A conversation is in progress; Inside a room in the Great House.*

2.5   THE PHANTOM OF THE GREAT HOUSE

DAISY Listen bwoy, doh sin yuh soul for this sex-starved, dried-up woman, eh. Let her pine for she husband by herself. If he prefer to be Don Juan around the town, instead of bein' with his wife; is his business, and not yuh problem.

CHRISTOPHER *(smiling widely coyly)* Look aunty, she's my employer and she give me orders, so ah have to obey them!

DAISY Doh be a fool for nobody, or maybe yuh think yuh **is** some kinda *Don Juan* too. Every day, like clockwork, everybody witnessin' the shame with of yuh cavortin' in the bushes with Mrs McDonald, like yuh turn bazodee. Watch yuhself eh!

(Spotlight fades)

PAPA BOIS Yes, I remember his name man, Christopher Bissessar – a dry-dry, tall Coolie man from up Gutt? Every day they would come out into the woods, regular as clockwork, 11am, and would stay for the whole day, till evenin' time. Then they go back home, just before her husband reach home, pretendin' to be very innocent.

FROG Eh-eh, she was a cradle snatcher then! What a wicked, depraved man-eater; poor Christopher!

PAPA BOIS She was an experienced woman, who used to pretend she wanted Christopher to show her their estate. She even went and brought 2 horses for them to ride in the estate, the way she and her husband used to do, in their early days on this island.

CRICKET So things was OK between she and the husband at the start then?

ANANCY Yeh man, they used to have other Estate Owners come over, then drink and fete and play music, y'know, living life like all Backra Beke used to; all over this island. And so, it meant the white

2.5   THE PHANTOM OF THE GREAT HOUSE

                people just kept themselves to themselves. But once they started movin' back to England, the McDonalds remained on the island, and so they were alone. The thing is, they didn't have any other friends to show off with, so old man McDonald, started makin' friends with the locals, especially the women of the town.

PAPA BOIS   Well, the time Mrs McDonald trapped Christopher was a time that she and her husband were almost strangers under the same roof. That Great House was just like a hotel room to him, and a prison for her. It was a place that he came back to at nights, after leavin' first thing in the mornin'. There was hardly any contact between them.

FROG   They say his daily life became one of drinkin' strong rum, chasin' after women, and living the life of Riley, as they say. And you know, it's really surprisin' how he grow to handle the River Antoine fire-water, in the hot sun, just like a rum jumbie! Jus' take a look at how cantankerous that man was!

FLASHBACK: *(Inside the Great House. McDonald is drunk, singing and shouting)*

MCDONALD   And what does a man have to do to get a drink in this place! Daisy! Ruth! Get me a drink this minute!
(Enter Daisy, Ruth, and Mrs. McDonald in night clothes)

DAISY   Yes, sah, it comin' right now! *(whispers to Ruth)* Go and bring the bottle of rum, another long night!

RUTH   *(whispers)* Yes, drunk like a skunk! And is more trouble he go make here again, tonight.

MRS MCDONALD *(angrily)* George McDonald! it's 2 o'clock in the morning! You're making a fool of yourself again,

2.5 THE PHANTOM OF THE GREAT HOUSE

and disrespecting this household, just as you do every night. Shame on you, to have fallen so low, George! You're no different than the poorest, drunken, peasant in this place!

MCDONALD *(staggers)* Shut up woman! Who the hell are you talking to like that. *(He motions to strike her!)*

MRS MCDONALD *(angrily)* Yes, go ahead! Well, if that's all you can do to me as a man, then go right ahead and strike me! You're a bully and all bullies are cowards! When was the last time you saw me without being drunk in the early hours of every morning. *(Sobs)* You leave the house before I wake, without even a wave or a smile. You come back at this god-forsaken hour, every early morning, with the stinking smell of rum and the nasty smell women all over you! Then you treat this house as an extension of your local rum shop!

MCDONALD *(attempts to strike, the Senior women intervenes)*

MRS MCDONALD *(angrily & defiant)* Heaven forbid! As God is above, George McDonald, you will not strike me here tonight! A **real man** never strikes a woman! How many men did you hit tonight? I bet not even one. *(crying)* Because with them, you don't have the guts to! You're a bully and a coward George McDonald! I rue the day I came to this place!

MCDONALD *(swaying unsteadily)* I will strike any woman I want! And I have a whole town full of them, lining up for me; even to take my blows. *(Hiccups)* To hell with you all! *(shouting at the top of his voice)* Ruth! Daisy! gimme my drink now!

DAISY *(approaching)* Comin' right now, sah!

MCDONALD *(Grabs the bottle of rum and points to his wife)* Mary, get out of my sight!

2.5   THE PHANTOM OF THE GREAT HOUSE

RUTH *(Taking Mrs McDonald by the hand)* Madam, save yuh-self, yuh cyan reason with the devil. Yuh see, he have the devil in him and it's talking through him, with the drink. Come, Ma'am, let me take yuh to bed. *(Mrs McDonald sobs as her husband puts the bottle to his mouth, drinks without restraint, then slaps it on the table).*

MCDONALD Now, put on some music and bring me another bottle!

(spotlight fades)

ANANCY So, as things got bad between them, Mrs McDonald concocted all kinds of useless excuses, pretendin' to be interested in the land on the Estate, when clearly it's poor Christopher she was makin' a play for. She played the innocent damsel in distress, until she force Christopher to eventually have his way with her.

PAPA BOIS You know, as *Father of the Forest*, ah used to see them for the whole day, and every day, that woman was losin' her self-respect, as a madam of the Great House. Before long, the sensational gossip started to spread like wildfire, all over the place.

CRICKET It was the talk of every labourer, who did witness the bacchanal or see them make their play in the bushes. And everyone minded their own business because they didn' want to be part of all this cote-ci cote-la, so they pretended not to know what goin' on. I mean, in the end, she just didn' have any shame, because Christopher was treated as a surrogate husband!

ANANCY But let's give Jack his Jacket, eh. We cyan blame Christopher too much. That man was just an employee; a labourer with muscles, a big strong body she could use. You could say as his employer, Mrs McDonald, abused him. She used her position to force him to obey her every wish. She's the one who took advantage of the poor bwoy; singlin' him out as a private jackass to ride her, behind her husband back, and right under his nose, in his own land!

FLASHBACK: *(Waiting for Christopher's arrival, at the workers entrance to the Great House, fanning herself from the heat, wearing a red dress, red sandals, and red lipstick)*

MRS. MCDONALD Good morning, Daisy, what a fine morning it is today, and I simply can't sit inside that house like a sauna, and deal with the flies. Fetch me Christopher! Today, he will take me around the Estate. I want to see the land and all the good fruits he's always bringing for me.

DAISY Yes, Ma'm I'll send for him straight away!

[Exits

(Christopher enters in short sleeved shirt opened at the front showing his bare chest)

CHRISTOPHER Mornin' Madam. Ready for what you want madam.

MRS MCDONALD Oh good, then I'm ready to go, and today we'll take two horses.

DAISY *(Enters, with an umbrella)* Here, Madam, take this umbrella you will need it to shade yuh from the hot sun today. Here is some cold water too. *(frowning at Christopher)* Easy to get really thirsty out there, especially being out for a long time.

MRS MCDONALD Thanks Daisy, you always know what's best. Then I'd say we are ready. Come Christopher!

CHRISTOPHER Yes Madam, I'm coming!

DAISY *(Aside)* Look at that child-predator. I tell yuh I'm no Madam, but she have no self-respec'. *(shakes her head)* Look at that poor bwoy.

2.5 THE PHANTOM OF THE GREAT HOUSE

Well, all ah can see is trouble ahead.

(Spotlight fades)

CRICKET Papa mwen, ça c'est comess, oui! You know what proverb say, What's sauce for the goose, is sauce for the gander! Or maybe she wanted to make the white man jealous.

FROG Well, for a long, long while McDonald had no time for his wife. Instead, he was sleepin' with every woman in town, only God knows if he didn't catch the clap. Because ah hear a Dougla woman called Jane, had a good plan to get pregnant for him, because she did plan to blackmail him for big, big money.

ANANCY And on top of that, not only Jane, but Ivy, a tall-tall Indian girl from *Behind-the-Corner*, Claudette; a good-looking, round-face woman from *Paraclete*, and a red woman named Angel from *Gouyave*. All of them planned to trap McDonald by gettin' pregnant for him, and then blackmail him! Listen and judge for yourselves. It's comin' straight from the horse's mouth!

FLASHBACK: *(Spotlight on Jane, Claudette, Ivy, & Angel)*

JANE *(putting on very short tight hot pants)* Well, Is ready, ah ready for my white meat! Every month ah saying to meself, *'this month, is the month'*. Let him come tonight man, ah plan to get pregnant for him! *(laugh loudly)* After all, I'm his good-time girl!

(Spotlight fades)

CLAUDETTE *(painting her nails with Cutex)* Well, ah know he running around the town, but who cares? Is my turn tonight, ah making the most of him, with my long-term plan. Well, we all know he's already

2.5   THE PHANTOM OF THE GREAT HOUSE

                 spoken for, so you could say, I'm his bit on the side but he's a good catch!

                 (Spotlight fades)

IVY   *(looking in the mirror as she curls her hair)* The other women are old and hard. Look at me, I'm fresh as a daisy; a spring-chicken. Now leh me tell you, **my** meat is sweet! *(caressing her thighs)* Tonight, he go eat dark-brown stew chicken!

                 (Spotlight fades)

ANGEL   *(applying red lipstick)* Well, he promise to look after me, if I get pregnant. After all, he's rich and with me having our love child - well, I guess you could say, I'll have him forever. *(applying eye make-up)* Let him come, he's just a means to an end. Cha! You think ah want this old goat, as a ball and chain around me neck? Nah-Nah! *(she laughs!)*

                 (Spotlight fades)

ANANCY   They treated that man as the only cock that could crow in the place, and he really fool all of them. Man, he just relished all the attention; knowin' full well he couldn't even father a child! But back at home somethin' else was taking place behind his back! Sit back and let's take a look together.

FLASHBACK: *(Somewhere on the Estate under a tree)*

MRS MCDONALD Come sit beside me, Christopher, I can't bear the thought of you sitting all the way over there, and I'm here; little, lonely, me. *(she smiles provocatively and motions him to sit close to her).*

CHRISTOPHER *(he stands)* But Madam, I'm just a worker, a labourer, and ah know me place, eh.

2.5 THE PHANTOM OF THE GREAT HOUSE

MRS MCDONALD *(teasing him sexually)* OK, my young stud, who calls himself a labourer; as your boss, I am now promoting you from worker, teacher, confidante, friend to my lover – you know, more like my little Chrissy! And that's an order! *(sternly)* Come here now! Closer! *(She forcibly embraces Christopher)*

(Spotlight fades)

CRICKET So McDonald was like a big, white cat playin' *outside*, while a little, black mouse, was playin' *inside* with his wife! And in the end, the joke was on him because his wife was hornin' him!

ANANCY Well yes, the day his bubble burst, did come with a bang! It was the day he heard a gossip about his wife. Man, he drink and drink, till he was legless with the River Antoine rum. Then he had a big clash with a dotish fella called Ramgolam, another drunkard, at a rum shop. In the argument, the man wasted no time in tellin' him his wife was a whore for a young black stud, while he playin' *Don Juan* with local whores, who are all laughin' at him! Well, the catty-catty man wasn't all that drunk because after he confronted Ramgolam, he stormed out the bar in a fury, to go home and confront his wife.

FROG *(loudly)* Woy-oh-yoy! That serves him right, proverb say, want all lose all. He playin' he's *Don Juan,* while a young stud, thinkin' he was *Don Juan* too, was playin' with his wife behind his back! Hah, Hai! Well look at me ass cross, noh! He turn into a cuckhold!

PAPA BOIS The sad fact is, McDonald became like a bull seein' red, when he went home. They say he knocked his wife about almost senseless, in his drunkenness, till they had to call a doctor for her. The worst part was what happen to Christopher.

CRICKET So what happen to him?

2.5 THE PHANTOM OF THE GREAT HOUSE

PAPA BOIS   Well, McDonald sober up and kept away from the town for 2 whole weeks straight, while he was makin' plans to get rid of Christopher.

PAPA BOIS   They say he paid some very nasty *Bad Johns* to beat up Christopher and run him out of town. But instead, they beat him mercilessly: dig out one of his eyes, break his head, arms, and legs, mash-up his backbone and throw his dead body in the ocean. Let's see these assassins in action.

FLASHBACK: *(Three men lay in wait in bushes to attack Christopher in the night)*

1st ASSASSIN   *(whispers)* Blow out the touch man, I see him comin' up the road.

2nd ASSASSIN   *(waits in the bush then jumps out to confront Christopher)* So you is Christopher?

CHRISTOPHER   Yes, who want to know?

3rd ASSASSIN   **We,** want to know!

(All three attack Christopher; there is a great struggle, noises, flashing cutlasses, bottles, sticks)

CHRISTOPHER   Help! Stop! You killing me! What ah do all-you?

1st ASSASSIN   You owe that crazy white devil, for playing around with his wife. *(they continue to attach Christopher as they speak)*

2nd ASSASSIN   Ah doh want to know all-yuh business. He pay us already and that money is plenty for this job. *(Christopher lies motionless on the ground)*

3RD ASSASSIN   Let's finish him off man, we done get pay a'ready? We not leaving no signs to trace back to us, eh. Throw him in the back of the jeep, we go dump him somewhere.

(Spotlight fades)

FROG   Didn't they say his body was never found?

PAPA BOIS   Yes, some rumours say he was run out of town, and left the island for Aruba. Others say he walks the earth as an angry phantom, searching for his

2.5 THE PHANTOM OF THE GREAT HOUSE

	sweetheart, Mrs McDonald. Those who believe that say his ghost intends to take revenge on anyone who have anythin' to do with that Great House. In any case, that was the end of Christopher, because he was never seen alive again.
CRICKET	Wow! You mean to tell me they assassinated the poor bwoy! *(shaking his head)* Man, that's Mafia-style operation, you know. So, what happened to the wife, Mrs McDonald?
ANANCY	Well, my friends, that story is for another *lime*. It's time to take a drink and besides, ah hungry now. Leh we go, eh. *(looking around cautiously, whispers)* They say, duppy know who to frighten.

[Curtains

ACT 3 SCENE 1 – OBEAH WEDDING BELLS DON'T CHIME!

Little Chris visits Mama Lola for witchcraft help to force a relationship between him and Stella. Inside Mama Lola's house, she's sitting with her head tied in a red cloth, around a table, with a lit candle, burning incense and a crystal ball, Tarot cards, a money jar, a pen, and a writing pad.

	(Outside Mama Lola's house, Little Chris looks around nervously, then knocks on the door).
LITTLE CHRIS	*(she opens)* Good day, Ma'm, thanks for seeing me so quickly.
MAMA LOLA	Come in. *(she sits across a table and motions him)* Take a seat over there!
LITTLE CHRIS	Thanks a lot.
MAMA LOLA	Well Chile, you sounded so desperate on the phone, with what sounds like urgent matters. Did you bring the $250 I ask for?
LITTLE CHRIS	*(hands her money)* Yes, Ma'm, here it is.
MAMA LOLA	*(counts and puts the money in a jar)* So what can I do for you now that you are here? You need to explain everything clearly before I decide *if* anything can be done.
LITTLE CHRIS	Well, this time, is a lot I want help with Ma'm; ah doh know where to start, but it's like this. I met this half-white woman, and she is from England. We doh really have a relationship yet, but I like her, and I was wondering if you could make her fall in love me.
MAMA LOLA	*(raises her eyebrows)* Who is this person? What do you know about her?
LITTLE CHRIS	Ma'm, all I know is, she is from England.
MAMA LOLA	*(handing him a pad)* Write her name on this pad. You say she's from England, who's she here with?
LITTLE CHRIS	*(stammers)* No-one; there's no one with her - ah mean, she's here alone.

3.1 THE PHANTOM OF THE GREAT HOUSE

MAMA LOLA *(stares at the nervous boy)* Then, who's her family in this country?

LITTLE CHRIS *(sighs loudly)* Well, Ma'm, as far as I know, she's here on her own and she doh have family here.

MAMA LOLA *(a little irritated)* How you mean, she doh have family here, how you know that's true? So, what she doing here then?

LITTLE CHRIS Ma'm, all I know is, I pick her up from the Cinnamon Hotel and take her to the Great House and she tell me that she is the new owner. Since then, she hire me every day, she pay me good money and at the moment, I'm the only person in her life.

MAMA LOLA *(raises her eyebrows)* So you think you're the only person in her life? But you doh know her background.

LITTLE CHRIS Well, she say her family used to be the white people who owned the Great House. And now that Great House is hers, they left it for her, in a Will. She come here to claim it, so that means she must have money. Ah mean, she must be rich. *(animatedly)* And as she's single and free like me, I figure she must be a good catch to marry. *(biting his lips)* Ma'm, you know I always come and consult with you 'bout everything.

MAMA LOLA *(avoiding his gaze)* Yes, but you might be playing with fire here!

LITTLE CHRIS *(persists, for something positive)* But Ma'm, you know is not the first time I come here, none of the other girls you did work on, did work out for me and it's not because I haven't tried but ah think so far, this one is the best catch! My dream is always to travel to America, so ah think she could be my dream-ticket to go abroad and make something of my life!

3.1 THE PHANTOM OF THE GREAT HOUSE

MAMA LOLA *(waves her hand pointing to her crystal ball, Tarot cards etc)* Well, it's one thing to *think* things, it's another to *see* what my little helpers in front of us here will tell us. Let's start with her name, so you'll need to write it here. *(hands him a writing pad)* You sure she's called Stella? Stella what?

LITTLE CHRIS Ma'm, I don't know her surname, but I could check it out, if you want me to get it.

MAMA LOLA *(looking at the letters on the pad, she winces)* Ooh! Stella, there's a big, big story behind this one. There's also darkness here. Now let's see what the Tarot cards tell us. *(she shuffles and asks him to choose 3 cards)* This is **PAST, PRESENT** and **FUTURE**. Ok, first the **PAST** - I see here big, painful, heartache, big split, big troubles, big confusion, secrets, death and unfinished business. Now, what's in the **PRESENT** – *(shaking her head disapprovingly)* So Little Chris, I see from this here, that you've been a very naughty boy! You better tell me what you did to this young woman in that old Great House. Because I'm seeing from this card, it will result in a pregnancy!

LITTLE CHRIS What! Stella go get pregnant for me?

MAMA LOLA But I see here, she was **not** a willing partner in this act. In fact, she was unconscious, when you raped her. Isn't that so?

LITTLE CHRIS *(puts a hand to his mouth)* Yes, Ma'm, but oh Gawd oh! Is sorry, ah sorry!

MAMA LOLA Well, right now, she's in a state of shock and her mind's a little confused. She doesn't know clearly what really happened in that Great House. She cyan remember the exact details yet, so at least she doh know if you had anything to do with how she's feeling right now. Not yet, anyhow. But this may lead to very serious problems later on.

3.1 THE PHANTOM OF THE GREAT HOUSE

You know what they say, play wid puppy, he lick yu mout'!

LITTLE CHRIS Ma'm, I swear, I didn' for one minute, mean to take advantage of Stella, because I was knocked out cold too, inside that place. But suddenly, from nowhere, after I groped in the dark and found her lying there with her eyes closed, I felt a strange and powerful force enter my body in that old place; it was full of rage, anger, and violence, and I looked at Stella lying there unconscious, she looked so innocent. It was just the two of us and I confess now, what was done to her was very bad. And to tell you the truth, I swear, it wasn't really me doing all that stuff to Stella. I'm telling you, Ma'm, stupid as it sounds, my body was being used by a strange force that entered me.
(shaking his head) The person who did all those things to Stella was not me, not my power; ah doh have that kinda strength – you know, I really can't explain……

MAMA LOLA *(holds her hand up to interrupt)* OK, OK, let's see what this **FUTURE** card saying, *(she turns the card over)* Oh dear! This one clearly says, "Forbidden Fruit."

LITTLE CHRIS Eh! So, what it mean?

MAMA LOLA Well, there's too much darkness here, lots of barriers, the path is broken, no clear way. *(Looks furtively at his dejected face)* But, I think if anything going to succeed, it will need to have a lot of work done.

LITTLE CHRIS *(looking anxious)* But is *anything* at all possible, Ma'm? I want her to marry me, can't you do that? I want to stop her from going back to England. Can you do that too? I want….

MAMA LOLA *(holds up her hand for silence again)* Chile, you may be asking for the impossible, but I will see

3.1 THE PHANTOM OF THE GREAT HOUSE

	what I can do. You will need to come and see me again in 7 days' time. This is a big, big work and I'm telling you straight, it will cost you a lot of money, about $2,500 US.
LITTLE CHRIS	Yes Mam, *anything* you say, money's no problem. I getting good money now, driving her around, so I'll definitely be back here next week.
MAMA LOLA	Then you will need to bring me $1,000 US next week. *(hands him a bottle)* Take this, use it for the next 7days, without missing a day. *(hands him a small bag)* The instructions on how to use everything, is inside this bag.
LITTLE CHRIS	*(bowing repeatedly, as he goes out of the door)* Thank you, thank you Ma'm. I will follow your instructions exactly as it says. I'll be back next week, with $1,000 for you. Thank you, thank you Mama Lola!
	[Exit Little Chris
MAMA LOLA	**[ASIDE]** *(shakes her head)* Well, well, well - that young bwoy is a real kunumunu! *(takes money from the jar and stuffs it into her bosom)* He shoulda know what we mean when we say craven choke puppy! *(Pauses, looks at audience)* So what! *(shrugs)* That bwoy wants the impossible, but since he have money to burn, of course, I will see him next week! *(blows out the candle and exits her house)*
	[Exit Mama Lola

3.2 THE PHANTOM OF THE GREAT HOUSE

ACT 3 SCENE 2 - LET SLEEPING DOGS LIE

Daytime In Daisy's yard. Daisy and Ruth, past workers of the Great House are talking about a letter received from Stella, who wants to meet with them, to talk about the Great House. White spot lighting on the two women, who sit outside of a house, around a small table and two chairs, with drinks in 2 glasses; fanning themselves from the heat.

DAISY *(Ruth enters the yard)* Marnin', Makomè, howdy-de do!

RUTH Eh-eh, marnin'! marnin'! Well, ah deh, ah still have the *Sugar* and the arthritis bones tellin' me every day, it's more than time to take it easy!

DAISY Ah know what yuh mean, ah not too good meself, but God is good.

RUTH When las' yuh hear from yuh son in America?

DAISY Eh-eh! Well, is only 2 days ago ah get letter! He and the family a'right, by the Grace of God.

RUTH Well me, ah get letter too, but it's not from family, eh. In fac', is surprise, ah surprise, that's why ah say to meself, leh me take a little walk by yuh, and talk face-to-face. *(Lowers voice)* Because yuh know what they say, 'bush have ears!'

DAISY Ah hear yuh! So, what the letter sayin,' that make yuh come all the way up the hill here, stress yuh-self, and lookin' so tired and worried?

RUTH True! Look at me, over 80 years old, seen a lot ah t'ings that ah swear <u>not</u> to talk to anyone about, till the day ah die. But now, according to the letter, this person writin' me, ask if the two of us would talk to her 'bout the Backra Beke people, who used to live in the Great House on the hill.

DAISY Eh-eh! So, what she want from us that she cyan hear from anyone else? It's so long ago, and that place is haunted; bruk-up a long time ago?

3.2 THE PHANTOM OF THE GREAT HOUSE

RUTH Sese mwen, she want us to tell her 'bout the people who used to live in the Great House, but as yuh know, me and yuh did see a lot ah things that only Papa Gawd we mus' talk to about! *(Makes the sign of the cross).* Long before, ah did tell meself, Ruth, yuh goin' to go to yuh grave with all what went on in that Great House. But as yuh-self know, when coco ripe, it mus' burs'!

DAISY Yuh think we should spill our guts and say everythin' we know? And when she want to meet us?

RUTH Sese mwen, she say she's the new owner of the Great House, and she hear we used to work there over 20 years, so she want to meet-up with us urgently.

DAISY Ah was thinkin' we should jus' wait and see what she sayin', and we could decide what to tell her, when the time come.

RUTH That's my thinkin', too.

DAISY Well, ah agree, we could meet her. But let her do the talkin', instead of assumin'; so, let her spill her guts firs'.

RUTH Yes, because mek sure is betta dan cock sure!

DAISY OK, then ah go send a message back to her, to say we agree to meet her. Right now, she stayin' at the Cinnamon Hotel on Rose Hill. But, instead of comin' all the way up here, we could go and meet her at the hotel.

RUTH That suits me fine. Ah go wait for yuh message, and please doh come all the way up here again, Makomè, jus' send somebody instead. *(Laughs and sips her drink)* Look at us, we have one foot in the grave! Yuh cyan kill yuh-self, jus' to give secrets away to a total stranger!

3.2 THE PHANTOM OF THE GREAT HOUSE

DAISY Is true, this 89-year-old body, with cataract eyes and stiff joints, that mus' have a stick to walk, find it real hard to manage, these days.

RUTH Ah know, an' we done give enough of our strength to servin' in that Great House, now look at us!

DAISY In fac', ah prefer to sit and watch the world go by in me veranda, and doh have to t'ink about that place at all. Too much bad blood pass there, too much heartache, and as yuh well know, that place is *Mama La Diablese* territory; ah know that dead woman lookin' for she dead child! *(pulls her shawl tighter).* Il fait foid metena! *(shaking her head)* It makin' me shiver!

RUTH Me, ah wouldn' set one foot inside that Great House again, *(shakes her head).* Uh-uh, not even if yuh pay me! *(trembles)* Jus' thinkin' 'bout it make me feel cold too!

DAISY Anyway Makomè, at the same time, ah have to say now that ah come all the way up here, is glad ah glad to see yuh too.

RUTH Well t'anks, ah glad to see yuh too. My whole point is, they say sometimes yuh should let sleepin' dogs lie, but these young people nowadays, they like to go chargin' into things they should leave well alone. So, we'll jus' wait and see.

RUTH *(standing up to leave)* OK then, so doh leh me stay out here, it makin' cold. Ah goin' now, but we go see real soon, if God willin'.

DAISY OK Makomè, walk good, eh!

[Curtains

3.3 THE PHANTOM OF THE GREAT HOUSE

ACT 3 SCENE 3 – FATTENING FROG FOR SNAKE

On a veranda in Little Chris's house sitting around a table. Stella talks to him about her plans to meet Daisy and Ruth, past workers of the Great House. Secretly, Little Chris is on an obeah-mission to find out more about Stella. It's daytime.

LITTLE CHRIS *(offering her a chair)* Let's sit out here, where the breeze is blowing, and have a little chat. Look, *(pointing upwards)*, see, the sun's moving overhead, so we good right here, in this spot.

STELLA Thanks, O.K. we could rest, only for a short while, then must head for Town. I want to do some clothes shopping today.

LITTLE CHRIS No problem! I'm ready any time. Leh me bring us some ice-cold drinks. Ah make it already. *(Leaves the veranda)*

STELLA *(speaking loudly)* So, tell me, how you feeling now, since we came back from the Great House? That experience was too weird for me, and I'm still confused about what really went on in there.

LITTLE CHRIS *(returns with 2 glasses of cold drinks)* What were you saying?

STELLA *(Hands one glass to Stella).* Thanks. I was saying I'm still confused about what really happened in the Great House. Sometimes I get some real strange flashbacks but then, nothing of it makes any sense to me. Worrying and embarrassing at the same time!

LITTLE CHRIS Well as for me, *(hesitates)* …em, I don't feel anyhow. *(takes a furtive glance)* But you're right, that *was* a very strange experience in that place.

STELLA Anyway, I don't know when, but I plan to go back in there again; after I speak to two old women who used to work there. Somebody told me

3.3 THE PHANTOM OF THE GREAT HOUSE

	where to contact them, so I sent a letter, asking for a meeting.
LITTLE CHRIS	OK, that's good. Well, at least they're still alive, they could talk to you.
STELLA	*(drinking)* Hmm, That's a *lovely* drink! Made it yourself?
LITTLE CHRIS	*(smiling)* Yep, made it meself. And that's not all I'm good at either!
STELLA	*(takes another mouthful)* Hmm, there's a slightly bitter taste. I know, you put a little Angostura bitters in it, right?
LITTLE CHRIS	Well, let's just say, it's Little Chris special bitters, and ah glad you like it. Specially made for you, Stella, ….. em? You know, you never did say what your full name is!
STELLA	*(drinking, smiles coyly)* Hmm! *Special* brew, eh? I bet you say that to all the girls you bring here.
LITTLE CHRIS	*(smiling)* Well, I only bring family or really *special* people up here. And you are special, now Stella.
STELLA	*(more relaxed, drinks again)* Well, if you must know, my name's Stella Gregory.
LITTLE CHRIS	*(lifts his glass)* OK, Stella Gregory, let's drink a toast to you! *(stands and raises his glass)* To Stella Gregory!
STELLA	*(laughing, flirting)* Oh you're a typical flatterer! Trying your best to charm me, no doubt.
LITTLE CHRIS	Charm you? Me? *(nervous laugh)* But ah hear I'm a chip off the old block! You know, like my dad, who, by-the-way, I didn't know! But still, I guess I mus' be living up to his reputation.
STELLA	*(looks at her watch)* Gosh, is that the time already? I think we should get going, we need to get a move on. And before I forget, I need you to come and see me early tomorrow morning by 9 a.m. Afterwards, I want you to go and fetch the two old women, Ruth, and Daisy, and bring them

3.3 THE PHANTOM OF THE GREAT HOUSE

                                over to me at the Hotel. *(Stands up)* But before we leave, I must use your toilet, please.

LITTLE CHRIS   Sure, come with me. *(pointing)* It's over there.

[Exit Stella

LITTLE CHRIS   **[ASIDE]** *(whispers)* Let's see how well Mama Lola's special type of *Bitters* will work on Stella. The drink was really made using a love potion called, *"Drink me, must have me."* So, with 3 drops in Stella's drink, means Little Chris *must* have her! *(he laughs a wild cackle).*

[Exit Little Chris

3.4 THE PHANTOM OF THE GREAT HOUSE

ACT 3 SCENE 4 - THE MAD WOMAN IN THE ATTIC!

Firefly, cricket, frog, Papa Bois and *Anancy,* are *liming again, in the absence of storytelling sessions. They recount a tale of what happened to Mrs McDonald, mistress of the Great House. Outside in a yard, the group sit around in a half circular space, drinking, chatting, and playing dominoes. Blue stage lighting with silhouette trees in the background, in a night-time environment, with night sounds.*

FROG   C'm on, ah have a deck of dominoes, leh we shuffle them.

FIREFLY   Me, tonight ah go keep the score. Maybe I'll play a round later, because the night is still young.

PAPA BOIS   So you see what we're reduced to doin', playin' dominoes. Anancy look at us, man. Wha' happenin' to our 'Nancy stories?

ANANCY   Papa, these are meagre times. Ah really miss those folktales too but tonight, ah go tell all-you about the white Madam of the Great House; that Mrs McDonald, it's a real mêlée. They say she became a mad woman, after locking up herself in an attic bedroom, that was supposed to be her dead child's nursery. She pine and pine, until one day madness take her, and she jumped from that attic nursery window right down to the ground!

FIREFLY   Ah tellin' all-you, at night, she used to wail as if her heart would break. Once or twice, ah used to fly by that window and see her rockin' ah empty crib and lookin' wild like a ram-goat.

CRICKET   So what really caused this situation?

ANANCY   Listen eh, it all started when McDonald find out about her affair with Christopher, their worker, the one he did get Bad Johns to kill. He went back home in a wild rage and beat the hell out of her.

3.4 THE PHANTOM OF THE GREAT HOUSE

FROG They say, he knocked her about until she pass out cold-cold. And hear noh, he lied, sayin' she fell down the stairs and then had to send for the doctor, because he get scared when the old women servants couldn't revive Mrs McDonald. Take a look at what happened, listen to the big LIE; we know she didn' fall down no stairs!

FLASHBACK: *(Enter Doctor with his kit into the Great House. He examines Mrs McDonald in the bedroom and comes out to give McDonald the news)*

MCDONALD Well doc, you must take one drink for the road, looks like you could do with one. *(pours rum in 2 glasses)*

DOCTOR Well, sir, let's just say, after examining your wife just now, I would say there is real cause for celebration. I don't mean the bruises she got from falling down the stairs. But I'd say she ought to be really careful from now on; now that she is in the baby's way!

MCDONALD What you saying! Now that she's In what way? Doc, are you telling me my wife's pregnant?

DOCTOR Well of course, man, *(taps him on the shoulder as he makes to leave)*. Congratulations! You can now be a real proud father around here for a change! And let's hope it's a boy, eh!

(chuckles, drinks the rum, then leaves)

(Spotlight fades)

CRICKET Bon Je! That is comess! Ah thought you did say McDonald couldn't have children. So, who she was pregnant for?

ANANCY Well, who do you think? Is for Christopher - you know, the labourer! You can imagine when they say same knife kill sheep, kill goat. McDonald did

3.4 THE PHANTOM OF THE GREAT HOUSE

	seem to go crazy himself. He started hittin' those bottles of River Antoine rum hard, hard again. Their house was a livin' hell for both of them. When he became so drunk that he could hardly stand up, that sharp-mouth wife of his, used to taunt him and tell him how much a better man Christopher was, than him!
PAPA BOIS	Eh-eh! That's the worst thing she could do, because she was carryin' Christopher's child; a black child right under her white husband's nose; every livin' day!
FROG	Man, that is bachannal!
PAPA BOIS	Yes siree! One night I heard him all the way from out here. He stumbled in his drunkenness and cursed his wife so bad, tellin' her to get rid of her 'black bastard baby' before he pull it out of her himself! Well, teeth and tongue does meet, but theirs was deep hatred, and with the evidence growin' inside her belly, the man made sure to take his revenge.
CRICKET	So that's why he got Bad Johns to kill Christopher! But dey say he didn' mean for them to kill Christopher, just rough him up a little and run him out a town, or outa the island.
FROG	But we know better now. These Bad Johns take it upon themselves to kill Christopher on the white man's behalf. He must have really paid them good money to do a job like that. Poor Christopher!
ANANCY	As time passed, when the Madam realise she belly big for Christopher who just disappeared, she started self-harmin'. She stop eatin' food and walked around the place in a trance, like a zombie, talkin', laughin' and screamin' all at the same time. She used to pick her flesh with anything, even her fingernails. Her mind was

3.4   THE PHANTOM OF THE GREAT HOUSE

	going fast, even though the senior women servants tried to feed her like a baby; in her delicate stages of advancin' pregnancy.
FIREFLY	So the nursery in the attic, that she fully equipped, in anticipation of the baby's birth, is where she used to lock herself up. Man, that was her sanctuary. As she got worse, everyone was afraid she wouldn't make it, so the doctor was there almost every day; 'tendin' to her more often than he was in his own home!
FROG	*(slaps his last domino down)* I chippin' out this dominoes game. *(pauses and stands up)* So, you mean to tell me that Mrs McDonald died in childbirth?
ANANCY	Let's take a look and see what happened to her.
	FLASHBACK: *(In the Great House, Mrs McDonald looking forlorn, being fed by Daisy and Ruth)*
DAISY	OK Madam, it's time to eat some food.
MRS MCDONALD	*(shakes her head, walks around in a daze)*
RUTH	Well, at least leh me bath you and change yuh clothes. *(pointing to her dress)* This not smelling too good. And look at yuh skin, bleeding again. Ah putting this ointment, but yuh must stop diggin' into yuh flesh, so.
DAISY	Yes, yuh got to stop self-harmin' and eat; yuh got to be strong for this baby that's coming. *(Speaks louder as she touches her stomach)* Yuh know, the lovely, beautiful baby that is in here. Remember, yuh have to eat for the laughing, beautiful, bouncing baby here – what yuh want, boy or girl?
MRS MCDONALD	*(smiles shows awareness)* My baby? I <u>am</u> having Christopher's baby? *(anxiously)* But where is my Chris?
RUTH	Shhhh! *(whispers)* Please madam, don't call that name here. Jus' say it's yuh baby, Yuh hear me? Jus' say it's yuh baby! *(Mrs McDonald frowns and*

3.4 THE PHANTOM OF THE GREAT HOUSE

walks away) C'm on, just eat a little more, please.

DAISY Make her eat! She *have to* survive if we have anything to do with it.

(Spotlight fades)

ANANCY Mrs. McDonald didn't die in childbirth. With all that craziness going on in her mind and her husband's bad reputation as the suspected murderer of Christopher, both she and her husband rapidly became walking shadows of themselves, like zombies. McDonald lost face everywhere, no rum shop served him, and even the women didn't want him; once they found out he was shootin' blanks.

PAPA BOIS That Great House seemed as if it was dyin' too, jus' like its owners. McDonald seemed to be losin' his mind - peein', and shittin' in himself; he became like a meagre dog, a shell of his former self.

CRICKET Well, you know what they say, You can do as you like, but not for as long as you like. So, what happen to his wife?

ANANCY Well, unfortunately for Mrs McDonald, they say the baby died in childbirth. It was still-born, like it spared itself the trouble of comin' into their kinda world, it seems. And it was after that, Mrs McDonald started lockin' herself into the empty nursery, wailin' like a wounded animal, until food had to be left outside her door, because she became violent and stopped talkin' to people. Left in total self-isolation, locked up in the attic, and behavin' like a caged animal, she became mad in the attic.

CRICKET Man, that's the saddest 'Nancy story to listen to.

FIREFLY But the old folks say, McDonald met his comeuppance when, one night, as he was drivin'

3.4   THE PHANTOM OF THE GREAT HOUSE

	home, worse for drink, with one of his Estate Work-Hands.
ANANCY	As the story goes, McDonald was drivin' at break-neck speeds and tried to swerve to avoid hittin', what looked like an old one-eyed man in the middle of the road. Take a look at how the stupid man was dicin' with death.
	FLASHBACK: *(Sound of a car speeding with radio blaring)*
WORKER	Yuh mus' slow down sah, yuh drivin' too fas'. *(sways as the car swerves)* Wo-wo! Too many bends in this little stretch of road.
MCDONALD	Driving fast? Who's going fast, me? C'm on! You know how many times I driving this same stretch of road?
WORKER	But sah! Look out! *(screams)* A man in the road!
MCDONALD	Where!
	(car loses control and crashes into a tree. The Worker groans, gets up from the wreckage, and crawls to where McDonald is lying)
WORKER	Sah! Sah! *(He turns over the dead body of McDonald lying on the side of the road).*
	(Spotlight fades)
ANANCY	Well, the Work-Hand survived but McDonald died on the spot.
CRICKET	So, as they say, same knife kill sheep, kill goat! The things you do to others can be done to you, is not so, Frog?
FROG	Yes, it's true. And interestingly, that Work-Hand was the only witness to what happened. He swears the old man who appeared suddenly in the middle of the road, looked just like Christopher! Of course, after that scandal,

3.4 THE PHANTOM OF THE GREAT HOUSE

ANANCY: everybody believed because Christopher died such a horrible death, that he turned into a Duppy, to take revenge on McDonald. As for Mrs McDonald, losin' Christopher, then McDonald, as well as her mind, and worst of all, her baby, that sent her right over the edge, in her mind. One day, she just jumped from the attic window onto the ground below - boof! She died instantly. So, the three of them are buried in the grounds of the Great House – Mrs McDonald, her husband, and her still born baby! I remember those 3 funerals well. It was so sad not many people come out for the burials at all, especially McDonald's. Take a look at how pathetic it was.

FLASHBACK: *(a priest in a funeral setting. Only Ruth, Daisy, and household staff in attendance. Individually, grave diggers cover 3 graves, the women place crosses)*

PRIEST: Ashes to Ashes. Dust to Dust. And Jesus said, "I'm the resurrection and life. He that believes in me, though he were dead, yet shall he live."

WOMEN: *(singing)* "When the roo-ll is called up yonder. When the roo-ll is called up yonder. When the roo-ll is called up yonder. When the roo-ll is called up yonder, I'll be there."

(silence, a bell tolls, as the crowd disperses slowly)

(Spotlight fades)

CRICKET: So who would you say is to blame for all this?
PAPA BOIS: Well, it's obvious is the two, white people. They were too comfortable with all their money and *Big Hefe* lifestyle, their idleness became the devil's playground. McDonald drove his wife to implicate Christopher and the foolish bwoy fall

3.4 THE PHANTOM OF THE GREAT HOUSE

for their stupidness. Anancy, isn't that why old wise people say, Anancy rope tie him massa!

ANANCY Well yes, and they right too, because it means, *'be careful that you are not caught in the traps you set for others,'* and I agree with that.

CRICKET Man, that's why that Great House is so messed up! So, I don't blame anybody for not wantin' to go there. That legacy is an ominous one. Things are not always what they seem. That's why I said the poor woman who's comin' here to go and live inside that place, all the way from England, is another lamb comin' to be slaughtered. *(Shakes his head)* Poor thing, she coo-coo cook for sure!

FIREFLY Well fellas, finally, I come up trumps in this dominoes game, but ah sorry, I cyan say the same for those Great House people in this story. So, you see, it's true what old people say, What sweet in goat mouth, turn sour in he bam bam! In any case, compadres that's enough folktales for one night. All-you, leh we go home, eh.

[Curtains

4.1   THE PHANTOM OF THE GREAT HOUSE

ACT 4 SCENE 1 – MEETING THE PAST IN THE PRESENT

A reception room at the Cinnamon Hotel, where Daisy, Ruth and Stella will have a meeting. Stella is sitting at a table, in pleasant surroundings, soft steel-pan music is playing in the background. She is joined by two older women with walking-sticks.

RECEPTIONIST	*(arrives with Ruth and Daisy)* Madam, your guests are here now.
Stella	*(rising)* Oh thank you, and can we have some drinks please? *(addressing the two women)* I can't thank you enough for coming. What would you both like to drink? Receptionist, do you have a drinks list?
RECEPTIONIST	We have our House Special fruit punch or other bottled soda drinks, or mauby, sorrel, sea moss, carrot drink, Guinness punch, lime juice, orange juice, and so on….
STELLA	Wow, so much to choose from! Ladies, what would it be, from that lovely sounding list?
DAISY	Gimme the special fruit punch.
RUTH	Me, ah go take the Sea Moss. *(They all sit down around a table together)*
DAISY	*(holds her hands out to shake)* I'm Daisy, ah please to meet yuh.
RUTH	*(also holds her hands out to shake)* And I'm Ruth, please to meet yuh too.
STELLA	*(animatedly)* Ladies, *(touching her heart),* I can't thank you enough for coming.
DAISY	Well, ah glad to see yuh, an' is a lot to tell yuh 'bout the old Great House.
RUTH	Madam, ah hope yuh doh mind me askin' - yuh mean, yuh come all the way from England, jus' to ask us, 'bout the Great House?
STELLA	Well, strictly speaking, you could say that my trip is solely about the Great House.

4.1 THE PHANTOM OF THE GREAT HOUSE

DAISY *(smiling coyly)* And how yuh findin' yuh stay on our island, so far?

STELLA Well, I'm enjoying being taken around everywhere, every day, and I have to tell you I've been to the Great House too. *(laughing)* Didn't need a key, the place was opened. But my God, it's abandoned! And to tell you the truth, it's really dilapidated; more like falling apart. *(serious now)* Ladies, so, what really happened there?

DAISY *(hesitates)* So, yuh say in yuh letter, yuh the new owner, how come? Yuh related to the McDonalds? How so?

STELLA *(confidently)* Well, it seems I was the only surviving relative, and they, that is the lawyers of the estate, have been looking for me, for quite some time, or so they said. It was on account of my birth; so that's how come I am the new owner!

RUTH *(winking to Daisy)* Birth! Ah didn' know they had relatives in England, ah thought they couldn' have children.

STELLA Well, here I am, the only daughter of someone called Iris Gregory, who confirms, I'm the next of kin.

DAISY *(making the sign of the cross)* What yuh sayin'? Iris Gregory!! Well, as long as ah livin' and breathin'! Ah used to know her well, for truth. My Gawd, *(putting her hands to her mouth)* so, yuh is the little girl Iris have?

STELLA Do you know her?

DAISY Know her? *(hesitates)* Well yes, *(pointing to herself and Ruth)* We knew her very well.

STELLA Well from what I understand, many years ago, my mum had a sister called Vera, who met an English sailor here. He was on the island for a short stay. He fell in love with aunt Vera and when it was

4.1 THE PHANTOM OF THE GREAT HOUSE

	time to go back to England for good, Aunt Vera decided, she loved him too much to let him go. She packed her bags and told mum she was going to England. Mum sent me to live with her, saying I would have a better life than she could give me. So, I grew up in England, with most people thinking I was Vera's own child.
DAISY	Well, well, well! So wha' happened to Iris then?
STELLA	I don't know because Aunt Vera stopped hearing from her after a while. All I know is, she gave Aunt Vera a letter about me, asking her to keep it safely and as a secret. *(Ruth & Daisy stared at each other in disbelief)* Apparently that letter was a legal Declaration, which was kept with my birth certificate. It was only when the Lawyers asked for my ID they asked for the sealed Declaration, and here I am.
RUTH	*(nodding to Daisy)* Well, well, well! Chile, yuh doh know half the story. And as long as ah livin' and breathin', ah can tell yuh my faculty is still good, and ah know what ah see with me own eyes, not what people tell me!
DAISY	If walls could speak, chile, they would tell yuh what ah goin' to tell yuh right now, but before ah do so, ah want yuh to forgive me for anythin' ah was forced to take part in. *(she makes the sign of the cross over herself)* And ah believe only Papa Gawd should judge us for what happen in that Great House.
RUTH	Yes, we are good Christian people, we work hard and as both Senior Maids in that Great House, for over 20 years, we seen a lot of comin' and goin'; enough to make a big harden-back man cry.
STELLA	Hey ladies, ladies, please, it's not about blaming anyone for anything. For me, that's a lot of water under the bridge right now, but I do want to

4.1 THE PHANTOM OF THE GREAT HOUSE

	know how come I end up with this Great House, as owner of it, being a direct blood relative, and legal papers saying I am a next of kin?
DAISY	*(Eyeing Ruth)* Well, leh me tell yuh somethin' - yuh real people was the McDonalds. They were white English bourgeoise people, here, we call them Backra Beke.
RUTH	Yes, they bought Carriere Estate and the Great House from some other English people who owned it before them, Mr. & Mrs. Kent, also from England.
STELLA	Wait, are you saying my mother and father were both white people? How come? You got me confused already.
DAISY	Well, not quite both parents *(lifting eyebrows to Ruth)*
RUTH	Yuh see, the McDonalds were English people who had a lot of English friends during their early days on this island, until their friends one by one, returned to England, leavin' the McDonalds as the only white people around these parts.
DAISY	We could see how the loss of all their friends was havin' an impact on the Madam, Mrs. McDonald. Yuh see most white people came and go, but these ones decided to stay, without children of their own to occupy their time, in the Great house; with all the empty bedrooms – the place yuh could feed half the village in one go! Is not so Ruth?
RUTH	Well yes, yuh know chile, a man is a man, they like bees visitin' women like flowers here and there, paradin' like saga boys, selling foolish women love-talk, and trappin' them like flies.
DAISY	McDonald was white, so the women think he was a good catch, and everyone did their best to get somethin' from him, mostly a child!

4.1   THE PHANTOM OF THE GREAT HOUSE

RUTH   (*laughing*) The trouble is none of the women could get pregnant and that's when they realise he couldn' have children.

DAISY   So yuh can imagine, how Mrs. McDonald was feelin', when day after day, her husband sleepin' in some other woman bed, leavin' her to pine away in this Great House alone.

RUTH   So, to cut a long story short, the Madam decided to befriend one of the male labourers and turn him into a surrogate husband, for all to see. His name was Christopher. He was young, virile and obedient to the Madam, so she made good use of him in every way.

DAISY   She stopped pinin' for McDonald and instead, enchanted Christopher until she became pregnant for him. By the time her husband find out, it was hell to pay. The Great House became a hell-hole. McDonald became a livin' monster - violence, fights, threats, fear, tension; staff could hardly stand it. Many of them leave and even his pregnant wife, got a beatin' now and then, when McDonald got drunk.

RUTH   We were the most senior Maids in the house, so he gave us strict instructions, with threats against our lives, to swear we will kill his wife's baby, (which was yuh), when it was born. He told us we had to lie to Mrs. McDonald and say the baby was still-born. Can you imagine that? The man made us swear to become murders - a secret he wanted us to keep, till we go to our graves! So as a result, for every day we livin', our memory is fresh trauma; all these donkeys years!

DAISY   In the meantime, he lost face with everyone in town, he became a laughin'- stock of the place because he was the one playin' Don Juan and then he get caught by his own tricks.

4.1   THE PHANTOM OF THE GREAT HOUSE

STELLA   So you telling me what?

RUTH   So we tellin' yuh when Mrs McDonald gave birth, instead of killin' yuh, that night, Papa Gawd gave us an alternative to the big problem we faced. That same night, one of the teenage maids gave birth to a still born baby boy, so we take it upon ourselves to swap the babies around. We gave yuh away, Mrs. McDonald's live baby girl, to the young maid called Iris Gregory. The maid gave us her dead child and we swapped them around, we gave Mrs. McDonald the dead baby. That situation really seemed to answer Mr. McDonald prayers!

DAISY   And our fears, as we didn't have to kill a baby. So Mrs. McDonald's child, the baby girl, is really yuh!

STELLA   *(greatly surprised)* Oh my God! I can't believe it!

DAISY   Yes, Chile, yuh mother was a white English woman. Yuh father was a local young black man; who, through revenge, McDonald had him killed by some paid assassins.

STELLA   You mean I've been passed from pillar to post all my life, for my own protection and you first made this possible? Sorry, but I'm in a state of shock right now. *(rising up from her seat)* I don't really know what to say, but have you both to thank for my fortunes, it seems.

DAISY   Chile, is only one thing we want from yuh. Can yuh please forgive us?

STELLA   *(puzzled)* Forgive you? I have to thank you for saving my life. *(Hugs each one)* I thank you from the bottom of my heart. Thank God, you also survived, having lived with the monster, Mr McDonald!

RUTH   Thanks, at leas' yuh not angry with us. Ah thought ah had to go to me grave with all this heavy, heavy burden on my mind, all these years!

4.1 THE PHANTOM OF THE GREAT HOUSE

DAISY: We didn' tell a single soul and we regret that we couldn't even tell Mrs. McDonald; it was for both of yuh safety. *(wiping tears from her eyes)* She didn' even get to hold you once!

RUTH: *(also wiping tears from her eyes)* She pined and pined away, lookin' like a livin' ghost, and spendin' most of her life locked up in the Great House attic-nursery, that she did fully equip, ready for yur birth; despite Mr. McDonald's objections and threats to her life.

STELLA: *(Shaking her head in disbelief)* My Goodness! That sounds so awful!

RUTH: Ah doh 'fraid to say it, but it was tabanca that killed her. She really died of a sad, broken heart, pinin' away for what she thought was her dead child, loss of Christopher, and even now we really, really feel guilty 'bout that.

DAISY: That's why we were scared when yuh contacted us, askin' to meet with yuh.

STELLA: Goodness, although my mind feels as if it would burst right now, with all this shockin' past, I am relieved, because this has put a ghost to rest, or has it? *(laughing)* Because I must say, I didn't believe in ghosts before, but now I'm beginning to think there is something strange about the place after all, starting from the grounds around the house.

RUTH: Well chile, yuh should know that Mrs McDonald is buried in the grounds, so is Mr. McDonald and the still born baby, she thought was hers. Their graves are behind the house, on the left-hand side. As for Christopher, they had him killed but nobody ever found his body; some say his body was thrown into the ocean.

4.1 THE PHANTOM OF THE GREAT HOUSE

DAISY But ah hear some people say he appears as a Duppy, then disappears, just before anyone could fully recognise him.

STELLA What's a *Duppy*?

DAISY *(Laughing)* Chile, out here, it means *a ghost*!

STELLA So, you mean to tell me I've seen a ghost?

RUTH *(startled)* What yuh mean by that?

STELLA Well, I saw a man - tall, good-looking, dark skin, with a felt-hat on his head, with only one eye, staring straight into my eyes. He was outside my bedroom window, early one morning, and then Little Chris, *(My driver)* said he saw him too, in the grounds of the Great House, when we were trying to get inside it! Both times he just appeared and disappeared!

DAISY *(Hand to her mouth)* Eh-eh! What yuh sayin'? Chile, yuh know yuh just describe Christopher Bissessar, yuh father, to a tee!

RUTH Papa Mwen, cat ketch rat but he teef he massa fish!

STELLA *(smiling)* What on earth is that expression?

DAISY Chile, it's an old people sayin', it mean good and evil often come from the same source. We have many wise sayings in this island, to suit any situation and believe me, they make sense. If yuh really study them good; they have wisdom.

RUTH What ah go say to yuh is, chile, take good care of yuh-self, while yuh are here. Yuh survived so far, open yuh eyes, and look before yuh leap! *(smiling)* Yuh must know that sayin' at least. Even in England!

STELLA *(nods agreement)* Well, Ladies, what more can I say? Thanks for taking the time to fill me in with all these details. At least, now the puzzle-pieces are beginning to fit in a way that makes some

4.1 THE PHANTOM OF THE GREAT HOUSE

	sense. Please have lunch with me before you go, it's the least I can do right now.
DAISY	Well, the day is still young, ah wouldn' say no; so t'anks for the offer.
RUTH	*(smiling)* And it's lunchtime now, so is the right time to eat!
STELLA	*(signals a Waitress)* Can we have the lunch menu please?

[Curtains

ACT 4 SCENE 2 – LAUGH AND CRY DOES LIVE IN THE SAME HOUSE

A room in Mama Lola's house. Little Chris has returned as instructed, for witchcraft help, to force Stella to love and marry him. In the meantime, Mama Lola, who is sitting around a table, a lit candle, burning incense, a crystal ball, Tarot cards, a money jar, and a writing pad, is seeing an important government Minister; a client. Little Chris is waiting nervously outside for his turn.

MAMA LOLA (*looks at her watch*) Well, to get that big promotion Minister, is a big work. As you know, we've been successful with past promotions but this one is very competitive. Many people will be jostling for this position, not just here on the island but I could see some from abroad giving big stiff competition.

MINISTER (*anxious*) OKay, so we have to get rid of the competition, Mama. You know money is no object. How much you want for the job?

MAMA LOLA Well, as far as spiritual work goes, you know, this is big, big work, and we could begin as soon as you have $5000 US for it. That's how much it will cost to get rid of the competition in your job promotion.

MINISTER (*sighs*) As long as we go win it, that's all I care about. So, I will be back here in 3 days. If that's OK with you, I will bring half the money first and the other half in the following week?

MAMA LOLA Em, you must know Minister, it don't work like that. I prefer you bring the whole amount in three days and I can begin my work as soon as I have it.

MINISTER (*contemplating*) OKay, OKay, Mama, I still intend to be back here in exactly 3 days' time, with the money.

4.2 THE PHANTOM OF THE GREAT HOUSE

MAMA LOLA *(hands him a bag)* There is something in here for you to use in the meantime, the instructions on how to use it is inside the bag. So, leh we finish for now, ah go see you in 3 days.

MINISTER *(takes the bag)* Mama, thanks, and thanks again, eh!

MAMA LOLA On your way out, if there's anyone on the Veranda, please, tell them to come in.

[Exit Minister

(Little Chris knocks on Mama Lola's door and waits to enter)

MAMA LOLA *(opens)* Good morning, Chile.

LITTLE CHRIS *(enters anxiously, sits down)* Morning Ma'm, I did exactly what you said to do. And I have Stella's full name and here is the money you ask for.

MAMA LOLA *(puts the money in a jar)* Where is the paper with her name?

LITTLE CHRIS *(nervously hands a paper)* I have it here.

MAMA LOLA *(reads)* Hmm! Very strange, and I don't know why, but somehow I see you and this woman joined together. Look, this card is not a lover's card, but there's something that binds you two together. *(looking puzzled)* Hmm!

LITTLE CHRIS Is it good news? Ma'm, Stella seem happy with me these days. But one thing I don't like, she's always on the phone chatting long-long to someone in England. Every day somebody calling her, and I know it's a man; do you see any problems?

MAMA LOLA Well, there's someone there alright, not a threat right now, but someone's who's interested in her. It's a kind of ultimatum he's giving her. He wants her to go back to England or he would fly over here to take her back.

4.2 THE PHANTOM OF THE GREAT HOUSE

LITTLE CHRIS   What! No! We have to stop him! Who is he? She's not married. He mustn't come here! You have to work fast, Ma'm.

MAMA LOLA   Well, I can see she definitely wants to stay longer here on the island. Her mind is less interested in England right now. In any case, she will remain here for much longer than she planned.

LITTLE CHRIS   *(sighs)* Oh good. Enough time for both of us to achieve my goals.

MAMA LOLA   *(looks at her watch)* OK, so you continuing to use what I gave you last time?

LITTLE CHRIS   Yes, yes, I following instructions exactly, Ma'm.

MAMA LOLA   Good, so that should be all for now. *(hands him a bag)* Here's more of the same thing I gave you last time, until I see you next time – say, in 3 weeks, eh. Because I need time to do the work.

LITTLE CHRIS   *(hesitates)* So you saying a whole 3 weeks?

MAMA LOLA   Yes, in 3 weeks' time. *(She stands, and seems in a hurry to get rid of him)* If there's anyone out there waiting, tell them they can come in.

LITTLE CHRIS   *(rises to leave)* OK Ma'm, thank you very much, I will be back in 3 weeks.

[Exit Little Chris

MAMA LOLA   **[Aside]** You know, sometimes you have to hold your tongue to hide what eye can see; to keep the peace! It's not what *they say or what the old folks* say; it's strictly what Mama Lola's saying right now! Sssshhhh!

[Exit Mama Lola

4.3   THE PHANTOM OF THE GREAT HOUSE

ACT 4 SCENE 3 – DOH COUNT EGG IN FOWL BOTTOM

In Little Chris' Car. Daisy and Ruth, onboard passengers, discuss the day's unfolded scenarios with Stella, without realising Little Chris has more interest in Stella than just driving her around the island. He is driving them back to their home addresses, whilst they are fully engrossed in their tete-a-tete, all details are clearly heard by Little Chris.

DAISY What a day, eh Makomè?
RUTH Sese mwen, that old, long-time comess we can now bury it, finally! Ah got t'ings off mi chest; it feel really good, and is about time too!
DAISY Well yes, more than 20 years of burden! Look how the past does catch up with the present, eh!
RUTH Yuh know, is glad ah glad, that our little Stella turn out to be a fine-lookin' girl; refined and beautiful. Maybe a little whiter than ah did expect, but look how Papa Gawd make it; she came lookin' for the two of us – the saviours of her life right from birth!
DAISY Yuh doh see how she looking like her mother too! In truth, she's a real chip off the old block.
RUTH Well, after all, we doh have to feel bad about what we did to her at birth. *(Shakes her head)* If only Mrs McDonald, her mother, could see her now.
DAISY Yes, if only. But still, it sounds as if Stella find a nice-lookin' man, with education in 'e head, refined like her, with standin' in society too. That's good, so he can look after her with dignity and pride. Then she can make somethin' of her life and that Great House - you know, in a decent way; not like what her parents did.
RUTH Yes, their story did bring shame and destruction on themselves and everyone else connected to

4.3   THE PHANTOM OF THE GREAT HOUSE

                  them. Ah pray she go break that spell and curse from the past, and start afresh.

DAISY   Yuh know, ah hear from good source, that the same Christopher that get the Madam pregnant, did have a child too, with a girl call Gloria on St. John Hill. What a shame, that baby was born *after* they done kill the father, eh!

RUTH   Yes, ah hear that too, wasn' she name Gloria Flanders? Imagine that eh, the Madam have a girl-child that she named after herself, and the lover have a boy-child, and ah hear Gloria did call the child by the father name too, addin' to the comess in this place.

DAISY   Well is wayward they wayward, both of them – bringin' more motherless and fatherless children in this world! Jus' when all this lawless behaviour go finish in this island? Only God knows! S-T-U-P-E-S! Callin' their children, the same names as them; like they hopin' this doltishness will carry on, after them!

DAISY   Well, at leas' Stella will be turnin' over a new leaf for them. That new life will be with this Alex person – so the new Madam and her husband, goin' to be in the Great House!
(Little Chris, influenced by what he is hearing, accelerates, drives erratically)

RUTH   And that young man Alex she was tellin' us about, sounds jus' like the right man for her. *(turning angrily to Little Chris)* Driver, slow down, noh? What we do yuh? Firs', yuh drivin' us fast-fast, then now you brakin' too suddenly. Wha' wrong with you?

LITTLE CHRIS   Sorry, sorry, ma'm, my mind is somewhere else.

RUTH   Well, make sure yuh mind is on this drivin'; ah want to get home in one piece, eh!

LITTLE CHRIS   Yes ma'm! Sorry ma'm!

4.3 THE PHANTOM OF THE GREAT HOUSE

RUTH — Anyway, goin' back to Stella, wasn' it very mannerly of her to put Alex on her phone to talk to us; jus' like we are real parents. Ah really like that kinda etiquette. Yuh doh find such good manners around these days!

DAISY — It's true, ah have to say ah like Alex, the Fiancée. He is a good-lookin' white-man too, same manners and etiquette like Stella. And from what she say, he is a big-shot over there in England, too.

RUTH — And Makomè, fancy nowadays havin' a phone with a camera to see people you speakin' to. We cud say our little girl turn out well then. Ah feel proud, as if she was me own flesh and blood.

DAISY — So, come what may, ah look forward to meetin' Alex when he reach here. *(pauses)* In 2 weeks' time, she say right?

(Alex swerves towards the roadside culvert)

DAISY — Driver, how yuh slammin' on yuh brakes so often, *(jokingly)* Wha' happen? Like yuh plan to kill us before we get home today?

LITTLE CHRIS — Sorry, sorry, ma'm. My head not feeling too good, just now.

RUTH — *(ignores him, then animatedly)* Anyway, ah reckon with all the plans for work on the Great House, it should look like it was in the early days.

DAISY — Well, ah go pray for Stella to make a good go of everythin'; as long as God spare me life.

RUTH — Ah sayin' Amen to that too, Makomè!

DAISY — OK Driver, we almost there now, yuh could slow down some more. *(pointing)* Yuh can put us down by that Grocery shop over there, on the left-hand side. Ah want to buy some green figs before ah go home. So Makomè, yuh stoppin' or goin' straight home?

4.3 THE PHANTOM OF THE GREAT HOUSE

RUTH Well, ah think ah go make a little pass by the shop with yuh.
(Little Chris pulls over on the roadside, to let the women out of his car)

DAISY *(Out of the car, through the Driver's open window)* So Driver, Miss Stella say she pay yuh already for our trip today, so t'anks for the ride. But listen eh, that was some crazy drivin'. Yuh mus' slow down chile, life is too precious to waste!

RUTH *(to Little Chris)* She's right, eh. Yuh mus' listen to her! In fac', take a good look at her, she's nearly 90 years old, and still goin' strong! Yuh doh want to live long like her?

LITTLE CHRIS *(embarrassed)* Yes ma'm, ah sorry again, m'am ah will try better nex' time.
[Aside] Well, look at me arse cross, noh! After all the money I spend on Stella, you mean to tell me she have a white man in England, coming here to take *my* Great House and *my* woman!

[Exit Ruth & Daisy]

(Little Chris drives away, then stops in a quiet place. He gets out of the car in a rage - slams the driver door and drops to the ground, on his knees)

LITTLE CHRIS *(yelling)* Papa Gawd oh, how you cud do this to me? No, Papa Gawd, you cyan do this to me! Not after ah spend all me time and every penny ah earn with Mama Lola, to make t'ings right for me. *(punches the ground)* Now, not'ing's good! *(yelling, looking skywards)* Oh Gawd, t'ings really bad! These women, Ruth and Daisy, ah doh know them. They doh know me, but they know everythin' about me. *(Punches a nearby tree)* Jesus Christ! Gloria Flanders *is* me mother! *(bawling loudly)* Oh Gawd oh! Christopher *is* me father! That's why they call me *Little Chris!* *(wildness in his eyes)* That makes me and Stella, *sister,* and *brother!* Oh, Gawd Oh! *(Holds his stomach)* Who go help me now! What ah go do now? Look what ah done to me _own_ sister? *(falls to his knees wailing)* Stella is me _own_ flesh and blood! My life is cursed! What ah go do now? Oh Gawd! *(Gets up crying, acts crazily, and runs off)*

[Exit Little Chris

ACT 5 SCENE 1 – MOON RUN FAAS TILL DAY KETCH 'IM

A room in Mama Lola's house, where she is sitting around a table, a lit candle, burning incense, a crystal ball, Tarot cards, a money jar, and a writing pad. She ignores Little Chris' loud bangs on her door, as he yells, shouts, and demands to be seen. Emotional and drunk, Little Chris demands to be seen urgently, but instead they end up shouting, cursing, and threatening each other.

LITTLE CHRIS *(banging loudly on the door)* Miss Lola, Open this door! I know you in there, so open up! Ah have urgent problems!

MAMA LOLA [Aside] Since I wake up this morning' I see trouble coming. I sense something wicked coming right this way, to make trouble, but you know what? They say, trouble make the monkey eat pepper!

LITTLE CHRIS *(raised voice, talking outside the closed door)* Ma'm, I cyan wait for 3 weeks' time to come back as you did tell me! 'twill be too late. In fac', right now is too late already. Everyt'ing is too late and it's not right. *(continuous rapping on the door)* Open the door, I need to talk to you. It's urgent!

MAMA LOLA *(opens the door but stands in the doorway, hindering entrance)* Bwoy, wha' wrong with you this early morning, you crazy?

LITTLE CHRIS *(distraught & grovelling)* Ma'm, t'ings turn bad, please you have to see me right now! My life is cursed! You have to help me! As for the work, you have to stop it right now!

MAMA LOLA Wha' you talking 'bout? Which work, ah have to stop?

LITTLE CHRIS *(raised voice)* You know, the one ah give you the $2500 US for. You have to stop it an' give me back me money.

MAMA LOLA Eh-eh! Give back, what money? Whoever hear about giving back money for spiritual work?

5.2 THE PHANTOM OF THE GREAT HOUSE

LITTLE CHRIS *(yelling)* Yes, give back me money! Why you didn' tell me ah cyan make life with me own sister! She's my own flesh and blood, my own sister! Ma'm, you <u>did</u> see it, but you hide the truth from me!

MAMA LOLA What craziness you talking 'bout bwoy, you been drinking?

LITTLE CHRIS *(yelling)* Stop playing with me, you did see it, remember, *(Mimics her voice)*, "You join together in some way." Why you didn' just tell me the truth? *(Pointing to her)* You knew, but you was jus' pretending to help, for my money, and take me for a kunumunu!

MAMA LOLA Listen bwoy, watch you' mouth, eh! Doh come here disrespecting me first thing in this morning!

LITTLE CHRIS *(yelling)* Respect? Who you? S-T-U-P-E-S! Leh me tell you 'bout respect! Respect stay under the bed, with 'e two hands on his waist! Jus' give me back me money, you charlatan! Or everybody go hear 'bout this! And ah coming back tomorrow morning, with my cutlass. Ah coming for me $2,500 US, or you go see a real, real mad-man for sure!

[Exit Little Chris

MAMA LOLA *(shouting after him)* So you threatening me now! So you want to go mad, eh? Ha! Hai! Well, remember, laugh and cry does live in the same house!
(she slams her door in his face and continues laughing. Little Chris, runs off looking wild and insane)

[Exit Mama Lola

5.2   THE PHANTOM OF THE GREAT HOUSE

ACT 5 SCENE 2 - HANG YU BASKET WHE YOU CAN REACH IT

In the Cinnamon Hotel Reception. Stella and Little Chris discuss the next day's itinerary. They are both sitting around a table. Stella has a drink in front of her and is in good spirits. On the other hand, Little Chris, looking sullen, refuses to drink.

STELLA	*(pointing to her drink)* I started on one before you came, what will you have?
LITTLE CHRIS	Oh, nothing for me today, thanks.
STELLA	Not even a juice? *(looks at his face in surprise)* You know, you don't look yourself lately. Everything alright?
LITTLE CHRIS	Me, I'm OK, just little things on my mind. *(Attempts to perk up)* But hey, Little Chris, is a sorter-outer of problems.
STELLA	OK, if you say, so. *(Excitedly)* Now, I just want to go over the arrangements for tomorrow. Alex's flight is coming in tomorrow at 10am. You will pick me up from here by 8.30am and we'll drive to the airport.
LITTLE CHRIS	Check!
STELLA	*(excitedly)* After the arrival, we will go straight to the Great House, so today you will need to come back around 4pm and collect some things I have here, to take there. I will sleep here tonight but check out in the morning before we head for the airport.
LITTLE CHRIS	Check!
STELLA	*(excitedly)* Now, was there anything else, let me see. *(she looks excitedly at a piece of paper)* Oh, and I thought once Alex arrives, you could take us downtown, we will lunch there and then head back to the Great House.
LITTLE CHRIS	Check!
STELLA	So what's with this *"check! check!"* *(staring at him)* You know, you really don't look all that

5.2 THE PHANTOM OF THE GREAT HOUSE

	good today; like you haven't slept all night. You sure everything's OK with you?
LITTLE CHRIS	*(pretends)* Like I said, it's all good. You know, Little Chris is just *cool*!
STELLA	*(animatedly)* O.K., and I've told Alex all about you. He can't wait to meet you. Our deal is the same, you continue to chaperone us and as our driver, show Alex a good time around the island.
LITTLE CHRIS	*(concealing his sullenness)* You got it, ma'm! As I said before, never fear, Little Chris is here.
STELLA	*(animatedly)* Take me to the Great House later around 2pm; the work on the areas I've selected should be quite finished, and the place should now look clean and presentable. So, let's go and check it out. At least this time we can drive all the way to the front door! What a difference from the very first day we went there, do you remember?
LITTLE CHRIS	Remember? How can I ever forget! My mind's been haunted by that experience, ever since. *(becomes serious)* It's how to erase these things - now, that's my predicament. How to undo what's been done!
STELLA	*(jokingly)* Hey! Don't be so serious, the past is the past, it's the future that counts.
LITTLE CHRIS	*(thoughtfully)* Yes, you're right, it's the future that counts and I'm counting how ah go live with mine.
STELLA	Anyway, make sure you buy enough petrol, I mean gas, for the car; we have a lot of mileage to cover tomorrow. I'm going to wash my hair now and get spruced up – need to look my best tomorrow, for Alex.
LITTLE CHRIS	*(half-joking; half serious)* You know you always look your best, mam!
STELLA	Well, I've got to! Been vomiting these past

5.2 THE PHANTOM OF THE GREAT HOUSE

                    couple of mornings. *(Little Chris coughs nervously)*
Think it must be something I ate, that doesn't agree with me. Still, I'll get over it, need to be careful what I eat, instead of being too ambitious with my food choices, and the amount I'm eating lately.

LITTLE CHRIS *(coughs forcefully)* OK Miss Stella if that's all, I really need to leave you now. Have to go and prepare for tomorrow's BIG DAY, right!

STELLA Yes, it's a big day, and that will be all for now, thanks. I'll see you later.

                                                                     [Curtains

5.3 THE PHANTOM OF THE GREAT HOUSE

ACT 5 SCENE 3 – WHEN COCO RIPE IT MUS' BURS'!

Firefly, Cricket, Frog, Papa Bois, and *Anancy* are liming again outside, in the absence of storytelling sessions. They recount the Finale of the play. Outside in a yard, the group sit around in a semi-circular space, drinking, chatting, and playing music. Blue stage lighting with silhouette trees in the background in the night-time environment, with night-time sounds.

ANANCY Cricket, is a long time we doh *lime*, man. Wha' happen' dey, you fellas gettin' lazy nowadays. All-you stayin' indoors, like you 'fraid of outside, or all-you pickin' up bad habits like the folks with TV inside their houses.

CRICKET No man, is not that, we still tellin' tales but not to local people, is all these educated people from the university, inquisitive about we tales and occupyin' our time. They seem like they can't get enough of our stories. The other day, they had me tellin' tales like mad. They writin', they recordin', they questionin' me; man they make me tired.

FROG Yes, me too, I was approached to give my version of some stories, and they insist on callin' them *"folktales"*. So, me, I went along with them, tellin' them all the stories I could remember. Ah have to say, when they write it down, and read it back, man it sounded different, but it sound good too, eh.

PAPA BOIS Well, nobody come over to see me yet, so I wonder if they interested in Papa Bois forest folktales, you know, we have a lot of them too. Ah have me French influence to tell them about. Is a lot, *oui*!

FIREFLY As for me, I say nobody can tell our tales like us, but if that's what it takes to keep those stories

5.3 THE PHANTOM OF THE GREAT HOUSE

> alive, I say, let them listen to us for as long as they want to. Maybe they will go and re-tell them to the world for us. That way, more people will get to hear them, than just the old folks in the backyard around here.

ANANCY That's why I was tellin' all-you, we have to think big, and adapt to new ways of doin' things. Remember the Great House, how everythin' started right here and where it end up? A famous story in England. So now everyone know about the Great House, more than we could meet people around here to tell.

CRICKET I hear you man, but me, I just miss we people voices man. You know what ah mean Frog? The way we say things, the language we use, the old folks wisdom in the language, somebody have to remind people every now and then how things used to be. That's all I'm sayin'.

FROG I totally agree with you, there is a big difference, when someone is actually performin' it, you know, the voice have sweet meanin'; the body have sweet meanin' and we listenin', and we add a little meanin' to! But we could share the tales too, eh. Ah really doh mind!

PAPA BOIS Ok, in that case it don't matter *who* tell our tales, as long as SOMEBODY is tellin' them, that's all that matters. It keeps information about our tradition alive, even if it becomes a history lesson, it's still alive, if you see what I'm mean. The younger generation at will get to *read* our tales if they don't *hear* it!

ANANCY But fellas, fellas, why so serious tonight? How come all-you gettin' so philosophical tonight? Leh we eat and drink, play music and enjoy the endin' of the **Great House** folktale, man. I'm itchin' for us to let people know how it end.

5.3 THE PHANTOM OF THE GREAT HOUSE

CRICKET Well, it really was a mêlé of supernatural events, emotional trials, obeah hexin', conspiracy, assassination, naivety, and revenge in the cauldron, stirred by up double-crossin', hard-headedness, death, the Devil's seed in a womb, men with mysterious hunches and crazy actions!

PAPA BOIS Cricket, I think you summed it up just about right. You know they say, more the devil want, less he get. That was the greedy Little Chris. The stupid bwoy take it upon his stupid self to think he could have a total stranger, by trappin' her with obeah.

FROG Didn't it all backfire on him? They even say Mama Lola had somethin' to do with it.

PAPA BOIS Well, when he found out he couldn't marry his *sister*, and he couldn't get back the money he spend tryin' to hex Stella, he tried to attack Mama Lola with a cutlass one mornin'. But she wasn' havin' none of it. You should hear how she take her revenge on Little Chris. Let's watch her at play, noh!

FLASHBACK: *Inside Mama Lola's house, early morning, she's conjuring a spell on Little Chris*

MAMA LOLA *(reading from her spell book and chanting)* Come, my phantom spirit, released inside that stupid bwoy, Chris. Fly! fly! Quick-quick! Come now! I command you to block every path he makes towards my home today. Turn his wicked, greedy mind onto himself. Bend his sword towards his own chest and let him fall on it! Turn his rage into madness and confuse him, NOW! *(spins around).* North, South, East, West! *(gazes at her crystal ball and laughs loudly)* Look! *(she points)* See, the madness already start! Yes, my spell will rule his life from now on! *(Cackles)*

(Spotlight fades)

5.3 THE PHANTOM OF THE GREAT HOUSE

PAPA BOIS Ah hear Little Chris became a ragin' lunatic; tellin' people how Madam Lola, the Charlatan, had robbed him. So, the night before Stella's Fiancée arrived, the poor bwoy just couldn't take it anymore; he put an end to everythin'.

FIREFLY Yes, I saw the whole thing from where I was sittin' on a leaf in the back of the house. It was late so I was surprised when I saw a car drivin' up to the Great House in the dark night. Then lights went on and off inside. So, I did fly by to peep and what did I see, Little Chris pourin' gasoline all around the house, after he finished soakin' the inside. I watched his every movement. He had gallons in cans, like he'd been plannin' this for some time. He was half naked, talkin' to himself, cryin', jumpin' and shoutin' like a banshee.

PAPA BOIS Well, as for me, you know as a bolee tree, I was in the distance watchin' the whole spectacle, but I had to turn my head, when I see the mad man pour gasoline all over himself – from head to toe, then run inside the burnin' buildin' screamin' at the top of his voice! Have a look at what he did!

FLASHBACK: *(Little Chris, stripped down to his underpants is talking and raging, like a lunatic inside the Great House)*

LITTLE CHRIS *(wild and angry)* God knows, ah had enough! First, the English-woman come here with she posh, foreign, self, to come and take we Great House. Is not my fault what happen! I didn' know ah have a sister in England! I coulda been well off! I coulda travel! I coulda been somebody. *(Cries loudly, uncontrollable)* I blame that Mama Lola. That charlatan cheat me, and take all me money! Even a flipping Phantom trick me; use me body, like I'm a damn stupid fool. *(shouts loudly)* And on top of everything, now

5.3 THE PHANTOM OF THE GREAT HOUSE

Stella white man coming to take what little ah have left, right under me nose! Right in front of me! *(He sprinkles gas all around the building, shouting)* If I cyan have her and this Great House, then nobody will! If ah lose, everybody mus' lose! *(pointing and looking skywards)* And as for you, Papa Gawd, you shouldn' ah done that to me! All me life ah want to make it better! Just like everybody, just to make it better. But look at me now, what ah have? Nothing! *(runs around madly)* And because ah have nothing, nobody go have a damn thing!

(He douses himself from head to toe with gas and lights a match. There are screams, groans, strange supernatural noises, as the fire engulfs the building)

(Spotlight fades)

FROG Yes, I did see the whole thing too. I was worried about the water in the pond and my tadpoles, with burnin' bits flyin' all over the place, ignitin' the bushes in the grounds, we had to keep hidin' at the bottom of the pond.

CRICKET And being away from anyone for miles, that buildin' just burn and burn all night, right down to the ground; until not a single piece of wood remained. It was almost as if the Great House didn't exist before! The only way they knew *crazy* Chris was involved, it's because his car was burnt down to an iron frame, right in front the Great House.

ANANCY As for his body, there was no sign of a single bone, not even his skull. The Authorities just said that his body must have burnt to ashes. My question is, was he really burnt inside the Great House? And if not, where is his body?

CRICKET And what became of Stella?

5.3 THE PHANTOM OF THE GREAT HOUSE

ANANCY   Poor Stella. Apparently Alex, her boyfriend, didn't make the flight over. Stella, never got any information, as to why he decided not to make the journey over here and strangely he stopped all contact with her! They say she had a nervous breakdown when she realised, she lost Alex, and was carryin' a phantom baby. Worse still, is that Little Chris was actually burnt to cinders, inside her own *Great House*!

PAPA BOIS   So they say she became mental and ended up in a mad house, where months later, she gave birth to a baby boy!

FROG   Hang on, hang on, a minute! *(Teasing)* Doh tell me, she name the baby *Christopher*?

ANANCY   How you mean? Close enough though. She call it Little Chrissy! Apparently, she did go stark raving mad, when she realised she was pregnant for her own dead *brother*; who raped her, whilst unconscious inside the *Great House*! But hear noh, dey say from rumours, she's plannin' to build a very different *House*, right on the same spot where the *Great House* was. Let's listen to Stella now, as she lay out her plans to the two old women.

FLASHBACK: *(Stella vows to rebuild her life, the Great House and to disrupt the past ills of patriarchy)*

DAISY   So, tell me Miss Stella, now that all t'ings come full circle and yuh suffer so much losin' everythin' - no Alex, no mother, no father, no Little Chris, no Great House! It's really a bit like yuh mother - what yuh goin' to do?

RUTH   Eh-eh Makomè, I was goin' to ask the chile, the same question. *(turning to Stella)* What goin' to happen now? Whe' yuh goin' to go? How yuh go live, now that everythin' turn old mas?

5.3 THE PHANTOM OF THE GREAT HOUSE

STELLA *(triumphantly)* Well ladies, do not fear. On the very old Great House spot, I will build a new House. *(women exchange looks of surprise) (Nods impressively)* Yes, you can believe it. Me, stella, daughter of Mary McDonald, madam of the old Great House, daughter of Christopher, the man she loved that they killed, will be Madam of my own *House of Freedom*.

DAISY Well now yuh talkin' chile! *(To Ruth)* Makomè! Yuh hear that! *(stands up and claps excitedly)*

RUTH Sésé mwen, I hearin' her. She could do it on her own too, without a man; with God beside her!

STELLA Ladies, haven't you learnt enough from my story or your own life, in the old Great House? You were burdened with the threat of violence; you were burdened with fear, instilled by the man of the Great House. No one raised any voice of objection against his violence, against his vile conduct of sexism or against his oppression. Old McDonald took absolutely no responsibility for the protection of those who kept him alive, those who ran his home and those who ran his business. Instead, what he showed was scant respect for women in general; those in his home, including my mother, and even the women of the town! *(pauses)* But that is all the past!

RUTH Yes, speak Chile! God is with yuh, and I with yuh!

DAISY And me, I with yuh too!

STELLA And let's focus not only McDonald; I did not get a better treatment from Little Chris either. You see, obsessed with his self-serving obeah, what did he do? There's Little Chrissy to prove It; a product of his day of shame. Then, where is Alex - the person who calls himself my Fiancé? He expressed undying love for me. Where is he now? Did he get lost in transition? *(sneers)* Where's his

5.3   THE PHANTOM OF THE GREAT HOUSE

	loyalty and fidelity? The truth is, I'm offended on behalf of myself and all the women who suffered on account of their association with the Great House. I stand before you and now release you all from your past burdens of fear, guilt and suffering of yester-year, as you wait on Time; a reliable 'Master,' to heal you.
DAISY	*(Standing ovation)* Bravo! Bravo!
RUTH	*(Standing ovation)* Speak, my chile!
STELLA	Ladies, today is a new day, a new dawn. I believe that the proper path forward should be to make a difference for the women and girls on this island. Building my own House of Freedom, is a way forward; to reverse the irresponsibility of the past, with different ways of doing things. From today, women who were once cowering slaves, servants, subjected to sexual impropriety just to survive, and threat of violence; will stop. Providing a new and better model for the future, is my commitment! That's what I believe and that's what I will do.
DAISY	You see Makomè, it's really true that laugh and cry does live in the same house!

(Ruth and Stella applaud excitedly)

                                               (Spotlight fades)

FROG	Woy-o-yoh! Papa Mwen, that will surely be another story and a half, man!
CRICKET	It's a real 'Nancy story, in truth!
PAPA BOIS	We have to make sure these university people, record this one on tape, for sure!
FIRE	Yeah man! Let them keep we storytelling alive inside tape!
ANANCY	As long as people can *hear* it, it doh matter how it get pass on.

5.3   THE PHANTOM OF THE GREAT HOUSE

ANANCY   So, compadres, looks like we come to the end of the Great House story. **Crick!**

AUDIENCE & CHORUS   **Crack!**

ANANCY   The wire bend and so this story ends: well, at least for now!

[Curtains

GLOSSARY OF TERMS

ACT 1 SCENE 1

1. ***Cook-up*** – This is a one-pot dish that incorporates the ingredients you have on-hand in the kitchen. It is a thick soup with everything you want in it – e.g. a combination of pig tail, or pig snout, chicken, or fish, callaloo and vegetables.
2. ***Asham*** - a corn-based powdery dessert, made by shelling dry corn, parching it, and then grinding or pounding it finely. Salt or sugar can then be added to the mixture and it can be eaten dry or with water. A must for All Saints night.
3. ***Liming*** - a term for mingling, eating, drinking rum and spending time with friends. Having a lime is a socialising Caribbean pastime, especially among men.
4. ***mêlée*** – Sensational gossip, idle talk, or salacious news about the private affairs of others.
5. ***Hoity-toity*** – assuming airs, being pretentious, acting as if you're better than others.
6. ***Mamaguying*** – to tease in gest or deceive by flattery
7. ***Sweet-talk*** – like mamaguying, to utter sweet talk in an insincere way as a means to an end.
8. ***Sweet-cheeks*** – it was a term of endearment, referring to a beautiful woman, similar to the word *'sweetheart.'* However, depending on the context, it can also refer to a person's attractive buttocks.
9. ***Doodoo chile*** – a Caribbean term of endearment, meaning sweetheart, sweetie-pie, honey.
10. ***Chookaloonks*** – a Caribbean term of endearment, meaning sweetheart, sweetie-pie, honey.
11. ***Every rope got two ends*** – Every story has two sides.
12. ***Mama La Diablese*** – A devil woman who roams around at night. (See also No.20 in the ***Introduction Notes***)

13. ***Bon Dieu Papa Gawd** – (French Creole)* **(Also expressed *as* Bon Je!)** Oh God, or Oh father God!
14. ***Another one bite the dust*** – likely to experience a breakdown, loss, or great disappointment.
15. ***Crick Crack storytelling*** - This African folk tale tradition is well-known and practised within the Caribbean territories. Whilst some may vary in renditions, they are all variants from a common origin. One major characteristic in the storytelling is that it embodies performance. The 'Crick Crack' storytelling is a group performance in which the 'audience' participates in a close connection between the performer or storyteller and the audience. It presents an African format of a leader or storyteller and a chorus which is the audience, participating in a whole storytelling session. In other parts of the Caribbean e.g., St. Lucia, the storytelling is performed in French Creole or Patois and the Leader or Conteur, does a similar announcement that the story is about to be told, by calling out **"Crick!"** ("Kwik" in patois), to which the audience responds by shouting **"Crack!"** or "Kwak!" Once the utterance "crick-crack" is completed, the Leader/Conteur continues by testing the audience with riddles, to which they would shout out the answers, in a session of exchanges. After this the story is told. The audience then becomes a chorus that is not only listening but also commenting. Often the riddles and exchanges are about their environment or what is known to them.

ACT 2 SCENE 5

1. ***Comme ci, comme ça*** - is a **French** phrase that literally means like this, like that. In conversation it means so-so, or neither good, nor bad.
2. **"*The same stone the builder refuse, does become the head corner-stone.*"** – *A biblical reference, (Psalms 118:22).* In this context refers to what has been rejected or

discarded, can, in another context, have great importance later on.
3. *poppy show – (pappy show* also*)* - means to become a ridiculous spectacle, to be made a mockery of. The literal meaning is from puppet show, meaning being laughed at because they have done something idiotic.
4. *Massa Day done* - **Massa** (meaning the slave Master), is the symbol of a bygone age, slavery. An expression used to reproach someone to remind them that colonial days are finished, and old privileges and oppression are no longer acceptable (from a Public lecture by Eric Williams 22 March 1961).
5. *Comess* -From **French Creole** *commece* 'confusion', as well as from **Standard French** *commerce* 'commerce'. It means confusion or a messy situation, associated with slander, rumours and entanglement or muddled situations.
6. *On the grapevine* – an informal way in which information is shared, commonly used to mean 'unofficially' rather than through an official announcement.
7. *Bazodee* – To be head over heels in love/ crazy in love, you appear confused or stupid.
8. *Backra beke* – an **Antillean Creole** term to describe a descendant of the early European settlers, (usually French), in the French Antilles.
9. *Living the life of Riley* – it describes someone whose lifestyle is easy and comfortable, with little or no worries.
10. *Fire-water* – a local term for the very strong overproof Caribbean rum, containing 69 to 80% alcohol.
11. *Rum jumbie* – a habitual drunkard or alcoholic.
12. *Making a play* - typically means that you are flirting with someone with the intent to enter into a romantic relationship with them.
13. *Spread like wildfire* - especially news or a rumour when it spreads extremely quickly.

14. **Bacchanal** - is a term used to refer to drama or problems among people. It can also mean loud, noisy partying and enjoyment.
15. **cote-ci cote-la – French creole:** Used in Gossips, usually of the amusing kind or as an adjunct, and so on and so forth; etcetera.
16. **give Jack his jacket** – to give credit where credit is due.
17. **Papa mwen, ça c'est comess, oui!** – *(French Creole):* An Exclamation for My God, that is a scandalous situation!
18. **What's sauce for the goose, is sauce for the gander!** – Used to mean if something is acceptable for one person, it is acceptable for another (often of the opposite sex).
19. **Clap** – slang for Gonorrhea, which is a sexually transmitted infection (STI).
20. **Dougla** – *(like mulatto):* a person of mixed white and Negro ancestry in the Caribbean.
21. **Red woman** – meaning a light-coloured in complexion, brown, light brown, reddish-brown or reddish-white; usually from a mixture of European (White) and Africans (Black) ancestry.
22. **The only cock that could crow** - A conceited, bossy person; this expression refers to the rooster's proud strut about the yard, asserting his rule over hens and chicks.
23. **Horning** – cuckolding or committing adultery; having a sexual relationship outside of an official one.
24. **Bubble burst** – to receive bad news that ruins a person's happy moment or destroy their expectations.
25. **Dotish** – acting stupidly
26. **Catty-catty** – describes a man who likes having sex with many women.
27. **Woy-oh-yoh** – an expression of surprise, or anticipation.
28. **Want all lose all** – means excessive greed puts a person in danger of losing everything they have.
29. **look at me ass cross, noh!** – an expression of disgust, disapproval in an adverse situation.

30. **Like a bull seeing red** – to become angry and lose your self-control
31. **Bad John** – a ruthless gangster with a reputation for hurting people.
32. **Lime or liming** - a term for mingling, eating, drinking rum and spending time with friends. Having a lime is a socialising Caribbean pastime, especially among men.
33. **Duppy know who to frighten** – Bullies know exactly who they can abuse.

ACT 3 SCENE 1

1. **play wid puppy, he lick yu mout'!** – it means familiarity breeds contempt.
2. **kunumunu!** – **(Yoruba** *kunun, kuni);* meaning a stupid person who is easily deceived or taken advantage of; a simpleton.
3. **craven choke puppy!** - Greed will be your downfall.
4. **have money to burn** – being wasteful with money or spending money with restraint.

ACT 3 SCENE 2

1. **makomè** – **(French Creole):** A familiar term of address to a woman friend, especially of similar age.
2. **howdy-do** – how are you?
3. **bush does have ears!** - to warn someone that they should be careful about what they are saying because people might be listening.
4. **Backra Beke** - an **Antillean Creole** term to describe a descendant of the early European settlers, (usually French), in the French Antilles.
5. **Sese mwen** – my sister
6. **Papa Gawd** – Father God
7. **sese mwen** - my sister!
8. **when coco ripe, it mus' burs'!** – All will be revealed when the time is right.

9. ***spill our guts*** - to speak truthfully and share everything you know about something, especially a sensitive issue or a wrong one has committed.
10. ***Mek sure is betta dan cock sure!*** – It's better to be certain, than to foolishly assume something.
11. ***Il fait foid metena – (French Creole):*** meaning, it's cold now or I'm feeling cold for (**French** - *Il fait foid maintenant*)
12. ***let sleeping dogs lie*** – a warning you should not disturb or interfere with a situation, because you are likely to cause trouble and problems doing so.

ACT 3 SCENE 4

1. ***the night is still young*** – It's not very late, at night, there's still plenty of time to do more.
2. ***mêlée*** - Sensational gossip, idle talk, or salacious news about the private affairs of others.
3. ***Bad Johns*** – ruthless gangsters with a reputation for hurting people.
4. ***Bon Je!*** - *(French Creole):* An exclamation - Oh my God! Or Oh God!
5. ***Comess*** - From **French Creole** *commece* 'confusion', as well as from **Standard French** *commerce* 'commerce'. It means confusion or a messy situation, associated with rumours and entanglement or muddle.
6. ***same knife kill sheep, kill goat*** – The thing you do to others can be done to you.
7. ***teeth and tongue does meet*** – there will be arguments or disagreements between people, especially in a close relationship.
8. ***Chipping out*** – *(in a dominoes game)* – to play the last tile in your hand.
9. ***Shooting blanks*** – when a man has a low sperm count or is infertile.

10. *You can do as you like, but not for as long as you like* – Everyone has a breaking point.
11. *break-neck speeds* – doing something extremely fast.
12. *Duppy* – *a ghost*
13. *Big Hefe* – from 'El Jefe' *(Spanish),* meaning the boss or chief or an important person with a very high status.
14. *Anancy rope tie him masa!* – Be careful that you are not caught in the traps you set for others.
15. *she coo-coo cook!* – She is in great or possibly irreversible danger.
16. *to come up trump* – to do something successfully, often when it is not expected to.
17. *What sweet in goat mouth, turn sour in 'e bam bam* – what you find yourself doing that feels good or pleasurable, can turn to pain, when you face the dire consequences.
18. *Compadres* – *(Mexican):* A Mexican way of addressing or referring to a friend or companions.

ACT 4 SCENE 1

1. *a lot of water under the bridge* - used to refer to something that has happened in the past and is no longer important or worth arguing about.
2. *Backra beke* - an *Antillean Creole* term to describe a descendant of the early European settlers, (usually French), in the French Antilles.
3. *saga boy* – a term used in Eastern Caribbean islands to mean a particular type of fellow who is a stylish dresser, who dresses to impress, often called a ladies' man or a "sweet man."
4. *hell to pay* - means something will have a bad effect or may cause great confusion.
5. *donkeys years* – Something that has happened a very, very long time ago.

6. *Harden-back man* – a big strong herculean man; physically and emotionally
7. *Don Juan – (Spanish):* a common metaphor for a womanizer or a man who seduces women with his reputation for being a great lover and who has love affairs with several women.
8. *Tabanca* – means to be depressed about love that is not requited – love sickness.
9. *Duppy* – a ghost
10. *To a tee* – it means something suits perfectly or exactly; or something done accurately.
11. *Papa mwen – (French Creole):* an exclamation, which means My God or My father!
12. *cat ketch rat but he teef he massa fish!* – Good and evil often come from the same source.
13. *look before you leap!* - A proverb which means to check that something is not going to cause problems or have a bad result before you do it.
14. *the day is still young* – it's still early in the day, there is plenty of time.

ACT 4 SCENE 2

1. *Sometimes you have to hold tongue to hide what eye can see, to keep the peace!* - this means sometimes it is better to keep your mouth shut and not tell everything, in order to keep the peace.

ACT 4 SCENE 3

1. *makumè* *(French Creole):* also written as *Makumeh, macoome* and *macume,* is a familiar term of address to a woman friend, especially of similar age. It is used by women in the Caribbean to mean 'my best friend and close female confidante, the women who, by virtue of the depth of her friendship, has rights and privileges over my child and whom I see as a surrogate mother,' (or

Godmother), among other references. Then name expresses the intimate relations which women in the Caribbean share, it honours the importance of friendship. Richard Allsopp, in the *Dictionary of Caribbean English Usage* (OUP 1996), indicated the possibility that *maku* in Belize with the meaning 'midwife', is also derived from this word.

2. *sésé mwen* – (**French Creole**): means, 'my sister.' This is a familiar term of address between women.
3. **Comess** - (**French Creole** *commece* 'confusion', as well as from **Standard French** *commerce* 'commerce'). It means confusion or a messy situation, associated with rumours and entanglement or muddle.
4. *chip off the old block* - it means someone who is very similar in character to their father or mother.
5. *turning over a new leaf* – make a fresh start in life, start anew, following problems or difficulties.
6. *look at me arse cross, noh!* - means when you almost disbelieve the amount of problems you current face.

ACT 5 SCENE 1

1. *trouble make the monkey eat pepper!* – it means hard times can force a person to do or eat anything, if he is truly hungry; that's why even the monkey ended up eating peppers.
2. *kunumunu! - (Yoruba kunun, kuni),* meaning a stupid person who is easily deceived or taken advantage of; a simpleton.
3. *Respect stay under the bed, with 'e two hands on his waist!* – The reference here is to a potty being placed under the bed. The essence of this expression of cursing seems to be nastiness, rather than the meaning of the words. The suggestion is 'I have more respect for the potty that we piss in, which is placed under the bed for use, than for you!' A grave insult.

4. **Laugh and cry does live in the same house!** – The thing that makes you happy, could also bring you pain.

ACT 5 SCENE 3

1. **Obeah hexing** – casting spells or unleashing spiritual powers against a targeted victim or enemy.
2. **more the devil want, less he get** – means the greedier you are, the less likely you will achieve and may lose it all, especially if you hurt others in gaining something.
3. **Cutlass** – a machete
4. **Banshee** - a female spirit in Gaelic folklore, whose appearance or wailing warns a family that one of them will soon die.
5. **stark raving mad** – to go completely insane.
6. **Papa Mwen – (French Creole):** a familiar term of address between friends, meaning 'my brother' (sometimes written as **Papa met!)**
7. **Everything turn ol' mas** – when situations have become disappointing, messy and downright confusing.
8. **makomè - (French Creole):** also written as *Makumeh, macoome* and *macume,* is a familiar term of address to a woman friend, especially of similar age. It is used by women in the Caribbean to mean 'my best friend and close female confidante (also in Act 4 Sc 3)
7. **sésé mwen – (French Creole):** means, 'my sister.' This is a familiar term of address between women.
9. **Woy-o-yoh!** - an interjection of surprise, or anticipation.
10. **laugh and cry does live in the same house** - a Proverb which means, the things which make you happy, could also bring you pain or vice versa.

PROVERBS IN THE PLAY

1. ***Every rope got two ends*** – Every story has two sides **(p4)**
2. ***Give Jack his jacket*** – to give credit where credit is due **(p38)**
3. ***What's sauce for the goose, is sauce for the gander!*** – Used to mean if something is acceptable for one person, it is acceptable for another (often of the opposite sex). **(p40)**
4. ***Want all lose all*** – means excessive greed puts a person in danger of losing everything they have. **(p42)**
5. ***Duppy know who to frighten*** – Bullies know exactly who they can abuse. **(p44)**
6. ***Play wid puppy, he lick yu mout'!*** – it means familiarity breeds contempt **(p48)**
7. ***Craven choke puppy!*** - Greed will be your downfall. **(p49)**
8. ***Bush does have ears!*** - to warn someone that they should be careful about what they are saying because people might be listening. **(p50)**
When coco ripe, it mus' burs'! – All will be revealed when the time is right **(p51/p86)**
9. ***Mek sure is betta dan cock sure!*** – It's better to be certain, than to foolishly assume something **(p51)**
Let sleeping dogs lie – a warning you should not disturb or interfere with a situation, because you are likely to cause trouble and problems doing so. **(p52)**
10. ***Same knife kill sheep, kill goat*** – The thing you do to others can be done to you. **(p58)**
11. ***Teeth and tongue does meet*** – there will be arguments or disagreements between people, especially in a close relationship. **(p58)**
12. ***You can do as you like, but not for as long as you like*** – Everyone has a breaking point. **(p60)**
13. ***Anancy rope tie him masa!*** – Be careful that you are not caught in the traps you set for others. **(p63)**
14. ***What sweet in goat mouth, turn sour in 'e bam bam*** – what you find yourself doing that feels good or

pleasurable, can turn to pain, when you face the dire consequences. **(p63)**
15. ***Cat ketch rat but he teef he massa fish!*** – Good and evil often come from the same source. **(p71)**
16. ***Look before you leap!*** - A proverb which means to check that something is not going to cause problems or have a bad result before you do it. **(p71)**
17. ***Sometimes you have to hold tongue to hide what eye can see, to keep the peace!*** - this means sometimes it is better to keep your mouth shut and not tell everything, in order to keep the peace. **(p75)**
18. ***Turning over a new leaf*** – make a fresh start in life, start anew, following problems or difficulties. **(p77)**
19. ***Trouble make the monkey eat pepper!*** – it means hard times can force a person to do or eat anything, if he is truly hungry; that's why even the monkey ended up eating peppers. **(p81)**
20. ***Laugh and cry does live in the same house!*** – The thing that makes you happy, could also bring you pain. **(p82)**
21. ***More the devil want, less he get*** – means the greedier you are, the less likely you will achieve and may lose it all, especially if you hurt others in gaining something. **(p88)**
22. ***Young with guts like cobo***. Cobo is a large carrion feeding bird of prey. Here it is used to ***describe*** someone who can withstand great pressure and is unmoved by challenges and difficulties. **(p19)**
23. ***What you head lead you to do, you backside go pay for it***! This proverb means whatever actions you plan and orchestrate, be aware that you will have to accept the consequences of such actions. **(p28)**
24. ***Moon run fuus till day ketch 'im*** - means you can't run forever, one day you will face the consequences of your actions or misdeeds. **(p81)**
25. ***Hang you basket whe you can reach it*** - A similar proverb is, *"Don't hang your heart where your hand can't reach."* They both have the same ***advisory*** meaning: keep your goals within your abilities and means. **(p83)**

26. **Let sleeping dogs lie**. This proverb advises someone that they should not talk about a bad situation that most people have forgotten. **(p52)**
27. **Fattening Frog for Snake** - This proverb refers to a man who cares for a woman and treats her well, should be *cautious* that his actions won't go to waste by losing her to another man, who will benefit from his good deeds. **(p53)**
28. **Doh count egg in fowl bottom** - Similar to, *'Don't count your chickens before they're hatched.* This proverb suggests that you should not make plans based on things you are not certain of. **(p76)**

Books by the Same Author:

- ❖ *Gang-Gang Sarah: A Caribbean Sensation (2020)*
- ❖ *Shakespeare for Children: Macbeth (2020)*
- ❖ *11+ English Preparation Tests for the CEM Exam (2020)*
- ❖ *Phonics & Spelling Workbook 1 (2020)*
- ❖ *Rhythms of Life: An Anthology of Modern Poetry (2019*
- ❖ *Mastering Comprehension Skills (2019)*
- ❖ *The New Caribbean Folktales and Legends for the 21st Century (2018)*
- ❖ *English Grammar: A Student's Companion (2018)*
- ❖ *Vocabulary Skills for Students & Teachers: A Practical Learning Toolkit (2018)*
- ❖ *Woman of Destiny: A Calypso Novel (2015)*
- ❖ *Woman of Destiny: The Text Study Guide (2015)*
- ❖ *T A Marryshow CBE – Honouring Caribbean Greats (2001)*

Phoenix Study Guides published by Eagle Publications

www.eaglepublications.org.uk

www.ingramcontent.com/pod-product-compliance
Lightning Source LLC
Chambersburg PA
CBHW071629080526
44588CB00010B/1336